THE
INTERNATIONAL
COOKBOOK

THE INTERNATIONAL COOKBOOK

The best loved dishes of 26 nations

Presented by
Kay Stewart

Lothian Publishing Company
MELBOURNE · SYDNEY · AUCKLAND

For J.R., J.C., and A.S.E.

Many people have helped with this book. Not least of these are the countless people—in markets, restaurants, preparing food in private homes—I have observed while travelling. I have joined in meals with people whose language I did not understand, but I was made to feel welcome at their table. Their enjoyment of food and their warmth have all contributed to awakening my interest in the customs and habits of other countries. I am indebted to Elizabeth David for her wonderful books, which perhaps more than anything else have made me aware of the pleasures of food. Similarly, the books and articles of Margaret Costa, Caroline Conran, Katie Stewart and Jane Grigson have provided many hours of enjoyment as well as invaluable information. I would like to thank John Ross for his help and enthusiasm, Helen Duffy for her endless patience and skill as an editor, Earl Carter for his beautiful photographs and Sandra Nobes for her excellent design. The following people have contributed in ways too numerous to mention: Sandra Symons, Sue McCulloch, Barbara Kenny, Leslie Tan, Lynne Wenig, Sue Wolley, Elsie Burrage, Tony Picnic, Anna Maltar, Judith Womersley, Dieter Czerwon, Harry Pill, Max Kay, Ricky Hoogenboom, Val Alexeeff, and Mr de Lemos of the Cafe Lisboa in Melbourne. Thanks to Market Import in South Yarra, Victoria, for supplying many of the props used in the photographs and to the various embassies and consulates who were so helpful in providing me with information and checking facts. Finally to Julian, Julia and Alex for their tasting and testing and patience (at most times), thankyou.

First published 1986
by Lothian Publishing Company Pty Ltd
Produced by Ross Publishers

© Kay Stewart 1986
Illustrations by Kay Stewart
Photography by Earl Carter

National Library of Australia
Cataloguing-in-Publication data

Stewart, Kay.
    The international cookbook.

    Includes index.
    ISBN 0 85091 242 3.
    1. Cookery, International. I. Title.
641.59

Editorial and design services by Elm Grove Press
and Sandra Nobes Design
Typeset and printed in Hong Kong through Bookbuilders Ltd

C O N T E N T S

G L O S S A R Y

Listed below are a few general terms, and some specific ingredients used in Japanese and Indian cooking.

bouquet garni: A small bunch of herbs used as a flavouring for casseroles, soups, etc., usually containing a bay leaf, a couple of sprigs of parsley and a sprig of thyme. The herbs are tied together with a piece of thread so they can be removed before the dish is served.

dahl: An Indian lentil purée, of which there are many varieties. In northern India it is usually thick, while in the south it has a liquid consistency.

daikon: Japanese radish, resembling a large white carrot, available in markets and stores selling Japanese and Asian groceries.

dashi: Fish stock used as a base for many Japanese soups. It is available in a powder form and water is added to make the required strength.

double boiler: Two saucepans, the top one fitting inside the bottom one which has simmering water in it. Sauces, custards, etc., that are not to boil during the cooking process, are heated in the top saucepan. A satisfactory substitute is a heatproof bowl sitting in a saucepan, as long as the bottom of the bowl does not touch the boiling water.

ghee: A type of clarified butter widely used in Indian cooking. It has an advantage over butter in that it does not burn or splutter. It is sold in tins and is available at supermarkets and stores specialising in Asian goods.

mirin: A sweet Japanese rice wine used only in cooking.

sake: Fortified Japanese rice wine, used both for drinking (warmed slightly and served in small porcelain cups) and for cooking.

shōyu: Japanese soy sauce, made from soya beans; it differs from the Chinese variety in that it is lighter and of a thinner consistency.

steamer: An aluminium basin with a clip-on lid, used for steaming puddings and pies.

tōfu: Bean curd made from soya beans. It has a delicate flavour and a silky texture.

wasabi: Japanese horseradish, available in a powder and a paste; different from the horseradish known to Westerners.

To cook well and to enjoy it, can be one of life's great joys. This book presents a selection of tasty and colourful favourite dishes from around the world, most requiring only a minimum of skill and effort to prepare. The best dishes are not necessarily the most elaborate or the most expensive but they will always reflect the care that has gone into planning, preparation and presentation.

To experience food in its country of origin, whether in a market, restaurant, or perhaps best of all in a family home, is always illuminating; the attitude towards food can teach so much about a country and its people. Markets in countries such as India and Burma, which rely heavily on spices in their cooking, provide an exciting spectacle with their mounds of gold, red and umber powders and a selection of mysterious fresh and dried ingredients.

In many countries food is treated very seriously and mealtimes are an important focus of family and social life. The French for example, do nothing in a half-hearted manner where food is concerned. From the croissants and coffee that start the day to the evening meal, everything will have been chosen, cooked and presented with the utmost care.

The harsh climate of many northern European countries leads to hearty fare and plates are often filled to capacity with food that is warming and filling as well as nourishing. In contrast, Thai and Japanese food, meticulously prepared, comes in delicate servings and presentation is considered almost as an art form.

The cuisine of different lands often holds surprises for the Western palate; sheep's eyes, rancid lard and fried grasshoppers take a little getting used to but the attention lavished on the guest more than compensates for the strangeness of the tastes.

Although it has not always been possible to achieve complete national authenticity for all recipes, especially where the names and styles of dishes vary within the country of origin, every effort has been made to do so. Above all, this book aims to provide both those who prepare the food and those who eat it with many hours of pleasure.

Austrian cuisine is renowned for its superb desserts. The famous Viennese pastry was first made in the 17th century and no visit to this elegant and sophisticated city can be complete without sampling the delicious strudels filled with fruit, nuts, spices and sometimes even cheese. Other sweet treats include Salzburger Nockerln, *a soufflé-type dessert flavoured with lemon rind, and* Sachertorte, *a Viennese chocolate cake, filled with apricot jam and coated with chocolate icing. Pastry shops and coffee houses are an Austrian institution, the former offering a selection of splendid snacks, the latter the chance to linger over a cup of coffee, reading the newspapers provided by the establishment for as long as you wish.*

The peoples of Austria's former empire have exercised a strong influence on other aspects of contemporary gastronomy. Sour cream was introduced by the Slavs and paprika came from Hungary. Noodles came from Italy and have been adapted to local dishes. Dumplings, which are as popular in Austria as they are in neighbouring Germany and Hungary, often appear in soups and stews. Herbs such as chervil, fennel, sorrel and capers are popular and aromatic caraway seeds are a particular favourite.

Austria produces its own wines, although these are not as well known as the German and French varieties. Locally brewed beer is very good, as are the liqueurs made from fruit such as cherries, pears and apples, while the non-alcoholic Apfelsaft *is an Austrian speciality.*

BETTELMANNSSUPPE BEGGARMAN'S SOUP

5 cups beef or chicken stock
salt and freshly ground pepper
4 slices rye bread, toasted, buttered and
   cut into fingers
4 eggs
chopped parsley for garnishing

Serves 4

Bring the stock to the boil and season with salt and pepper. Place the toast fingers in four soup bowls and break an egg into each. Ladle the boiling stock over the eggs, sprinkle with parsley and serve at once.

LEBERKUCHEN STEAMED LIVER CAKE

This cake is best made a day or two before it is to be eaten.

250 g fresh breadcrumbs
$\frac{3}{4}$ cup milk
125 g butter
500 g goose livers, cleaned
1 onion, peeled and grated
2 tablespoons chopped parsley
$1\frac{1}{4}$ cups cream
6 eggs, well beaten
salt and pepper
plain flour

Serves 6

Soak the breadcrumbs in the milk. Melt the butter in a pan, add the livers and cook for about 10 minutes over a gentle heat. Remove the livers, allow to cool and then mince. Put in the grated onion and the milky breadcrumbs and stir well. Add the parsley, cream and the well beaten eggs and season with salt and pepper.

Butter a steamer, sprinkle with a little flour and add the liver mixture. Cover with several layers of waxed paper before securing the lid firmly. Steam for $1\frac{1}{2}$ hours. Let the mixture cool before removing it from the steamer. If it is not to be used immediately, cover with clean waxed paper, replace the lid and store in the steamer. To serve, slice thinly.

ROHER SALAT IN SAUERRAHM DANDELION LEAVES IN SOUR CREAM

Dandelions are often regarded as purely garden weeds. In certain European countries, however, they are used in salads, or as in this recipe they are served with a sour cream dressing, as a vegetable accompaniment to a main course.

1 large bunch dandelion leaves
   (about 500 g)
boiling water
$\frac{1}{4}$ cup water
salt
$\frac{3}{4}$ cup sour cream
freshly ground black pepper
$\frac{1}{2}$ teaspoon paprika

Serves 4

Plunge the dandelion leaves into a sink of cold water and wash thoroughly. Put them into a large bowl, cover with boiling water and drain.

Put $\frac{1}{4}$ cup water in the bottom of a large pan, add salt, and bring to the boil. Add the leaves, cover the pan, and simmer for 10 minutes, shaking the pan from time to time. Drain and chop the leaves coarsely.

Heat the sour cream in a medium-sized pan, add the leaves, stir and season with salt and pepper. When the cream is just beginning to bubble remove it from the stove, place in a serving dish and sprinkle with paprika.

AUSTRIA

KASSELER MIT TOMATENSOSSE

SMOKED PORK WITH A SAUCE
OF TOMATOES

*Kasseler is the smoked loin of pork, and should
be available from continental butchers and
delicatessens. Ask the butcher to remove the
rind.*

**piece of kasseler (allow 2 chops
    per person)**
oil
1 tablespoon coriander seeds
1 tablespoon mustard seeds

Sauce
3 tablespoons butter
2 onions, peeled and chopped
1 kg tomatoes, peeled and seeded
**small sprig fresh basil, chopped, or
    ½ teaspoon dried basil**
1 teaspoon sugar
1 clove garlic, peeled and chopped
salt and freshly ground black pepper

Serves 4–6

Preheat the over to 180°C/350°F.
   Place the kasseler into a baking dish, pour a little oil over it and
sprinkle with the coriander and mustard seeds. Cook in a moderate oven
for about an hour.
   To make the sauce, melt the butter in a large pan and cook the onions
until soft. Add the other ingredients and simmer gently until the sauce is
thick (about 30 minutes).
   Slice the meat, arrange on a serving dish and serve the sauce
separately.

WIENER SCHNITZEL

VEAL ESCALOPES FROM VIENNA

4 large slices veal, paper thin
2 tablespoons plain flour
**1 egg, beaten with 1 tablespoon oil and
    1 tablespoon water**
fine breadcrumbs
salt and freshly ground pepper
butter
1–2 lemons
parsley

Serves 4

Dust each slice of veal lightly with flour, dip it into the egg mixture and
coat with breadcrumbs, making sure they cover all the meat. Heat the
butter in a large, heavy based pan and cook the schnitzels until crisp and
golden. Allow about 4 minutes on each side. Drain on kitchen paper and
serve at once, garnished with lemon wedges and parsley.

PFLAUMENKNÖDEL

PLUM DUMPLINGS

**20 plums (choose a variety which has
    seeds that are easy to remove)**
20 sugar cubes
2¼ cups plain flour
½ teaspoon salt
**4 tablespoons butter, cut into small
    pieces**

Wipe the plums with a damp cloth. Using a knife, make a slit in the side
of the plums and carefully remove the stones. Place a cube of sugar in the
cavity. Sift the flour and salt into a bowl. Add the butter and work into
the flour with a pastry blender or with your fingers. Add the beaten eggs
and just enough milk to make a stiff dough. Break the dough into two
equal parts and roll out on a floured board. Cut each part into 10 equal
pieces, each one large enough to enclose a plum. Wrap each plum in a

2 eggs, beaten
½ cup milk
salted, boiling water
2 tablespoons butter
1 cup breadcrumbs
2 tablespoons castor sugar

Makes 20 dumplings

square of dough. Pinch the dough together with moistened fingers, making sure that the plum is completely enclosed.

Have ready a large pan of salted, boiling water. Cook the dumplings, a few at a time, for about 10 minutes. Remove with a slotted spoon and drain on kitchen paper, while cooking the rest. In a small pan melt the butter and brown the breadcrumbs and sugar. Roll the dumplings in this mixture and serve immediately.

SALZBURGER NOCKERLN   VANILLA SOUFFLÉ

A light soufflé-type pudding dating from 18th-century Salzburg.

50 g butter
4 egg yolks
5 egg whites
75 g castor sugar
½ teaspoon vanilla essence
rind of 1 lemon, finely grated
3 tablespoons plain flour, sifted
½ cup milk
icing sugar for decoration

Serves 4

Lightly grease a soufflé dish and preheat the oven to 200°C/400°F.

Beat 40 g of the butter with the egg yolks until creamy. In a separate bowl whisk the egg whites until stiff, fold in half the sugar and keep whisking. When the meringue is of a stiff consistency fold 2 tablespoons of it into the yolk mixture. Then gently fold the yolks into the whites. Fold in the sifted flour and the lemon rind.

Heat the milk to boiling point, add the butter and the remaining sugar and stir until dissolved. Place this mixture in the bottom of the prepared dish, pile on the meringue, and bake for 12–15 minutes until pale golden and just setting. Sprinkle with icing sugar and serve at once.

SACHERTORTE   VIENNESE CHOCOLATE CAKE

According to legend this cake was first made in 1832 by Franz Sacher for his master Prince Metternich. Today Sachertorte is packaged in wooden boxes and sent all over the world. Whether it bears any resemblance to the original is unknown.

250 g plain dark chocolate
2 tablespoons rum
375 g butter
375 g castor sugar
5 egg yolks
5 egg whites
185 g plain flour
apricot jam

Icing
125 g plain chocolate
4 tablespoons icing sugar
6 tablespoons water

Serves 6–8

Preheat the oven to 180°C/350°F and grease two 20-cm cake tins.

Place the chocolate in a double boiler and melt over a gentle heat. Add the rum, stir and allow to cool.

Beat the butter and castor sugar until light and fluffy. Add the yolks and beat well. Whisk the egg whites until stiff and fold into the yolk mixture, simultaneously with the sifted flour. It is essential not to beat the flour or the cake will be tough. Carefully stir in the melted chocolate and rum.

Divide the mixture between the two prepared tins and bake for about 45 minutes or until the cake springs back into shape when pressed with a finger. Allow to cool. Release the two halves from the tins and sandwich together with jam.

To make the icing, melt the chocolate in a double boiler over a low heat. Add the icing sugar and enough water to obtain the required consistency. Cook slowly for about 10 minutes. Let the mixture cool, but keep stirring. Spread on the cake and smooth with a palette-knife.

Food in Belgium reflects the French, Dutch and German cultural associations of the three principal language groups, although it is perhaps most often compared in quality to that of France.

Seafood is presented in many interesting and unusual ways. For example, from the beautiful Flemish city of Ghent comes waterzooi, a soup and main course cooked in one pot, made from either fish or chicken simmered slowly with wine and herbs. Plump eels can be simply crumbed and served with a tartare sauce or sautéd in butter with fresh herbs then poached in a white wine sauce enriched with egg yolks. Mussels and oysters are popular, while bigorneaux (sea snails) are accompanied with a hat pin in a small pin cushion, to be used in extracting them from their shells. Trout are sometimes caught from a stream running beside the restaurant, ensuring absolute freshness.

Belgians like their food fresh; bread is baked three times a day while delicious waffles are prepared by street stall vendors and eaten plain or with fruit and cream. Markets are always a good indication of a people's attitude towards food and Belgian markets bustle with activity and colour.

The countryside provides excellent game including boar, hare, venison and pheasant, each frequently marinated in wine and herbs and then turned into rich and flavoursome casseroles.

Perhaps Belgium's most tempting taste treats are its chocolates. Looking like works of art, these appear in extravagant window displays of dark, milk and white chocolates made into a variety of animal, shell and other fantastic shapes, all tasting even better than they look!

WATERZOOI

This classic Belgian recipe takes its name from the Flemish for 'water on the boil'. There is a fish version as well as the chicken one given here, and it is a soup as well as a main course, all cooked in one pot.

1 boiling fowl (2½ kg)
200 g chicken livers
1 veal knuckle, sawn into several pieces
2 sticks celery, including tops, chopped
3 onions, peeled and chopped
2 carrots, peeled and chopped
2 leeks, carefully cleaned and chopped (use a little of the green top part)
3 bay leaves
2 sprigs fresh thyme or ½ teaspoon dried thyme
2 sprigs parsley or 1 teaspoon dried parsley
4 egg yolks
juice of 1 lemon
250 ml sour cream
salt and freshly ground pepper

Serves 6

Place the chicken, chicken livers, veal, vegetables and herbs in a large pot with a well fitting lid. Cover with water, bring to the boil and simmer until the chicken is tender—about 2½ hours. Meanwhile beat the egg yolks and add the lemon juice and sour cream. Season with salt and pepper.

When the chicken is tender remove it and the livers to a plate and allow to cool slightly. Discard the veal knuckle. Remove the skin from the chicken and cut it into serving portions, discarding any gristle. Cut the livers into pieces. Keep livers and chicken warm while preparing the broth.

Strain the broth, pressing the vegetables well to extract all their goodness. Skim off any fat, bring to the boil and simmer until it reduces by one-third. Take ½ cup of the broth and add it slowly to the egg and cream mixture. Now add this to the broth in the pot, taking care not to let it boil or it will curdle. Stir until it thickens. Add the chicken pieces and livers and serve in deep bowls.

PÂTÉ DE BRUXELLES

1 small chicken
200 g fat bacon, minced
300 g pork or veal, minced
salt and freshly ground black pepper
pinch of allspice
pinch of ground cloves
sprig fresh thyme or pinch of dried thyme
1 clove garlic, peeled and crushed
2 sprigs parsley, chopped
1 egg, beaten
⅓ cup brandy or sherry
1 bay leaf

Serves 6–8

Carefully cut the meat from the chicken, remove the skin and slice the meat into neat pieces of approximately the same size.

Place the minced bacon and pork in a bowl and season with salt and pepper. Add allspice, cloves, thyme, garlic, parsley, egg and brandy. Stir until thoroughly combined. Place a layer of this mixture in the bottom of a terrine or small earthenware casserole. Cover with a layer of the sliced chicken meat and season with a little salt and pepper. Repeat this process until all the meat is used, finishing with a layer of the mince. Place the bay leaf on top. Cover with a double layer of waxed paper and then the lid. Place in a baking tin and add enough water to come half way up the side of the terrine.

Cook in a slow oven at 150°C/300°F for about 2½ hours, removing the lid during the last ½ hour of cooking. When ready the pâté will have shrunk away slightly from the sides of the terrine. Remove from the oven, place a weight on top of the pâté and leave to stand overnight. Serve at room temperature, sliced with toast or fresh crunchy bread.

MOULES À LA BRUXELLOISE

BRUSSELS-STYLE MUSSELS

Mussels and eel are specialities of Brussels, and are presented in a variety of delicious ways.

5 kg mussels
3 tablespoons butter
1 onion, peeled and chopped
1 bunch celery (use leaves only)
medium-sized bunch parsley, chopped
1 cup white wine
freshly ground black pepper

Serves 4

The most important thing to remember when cooking mussels is that they must be thoroughly cleaned. First, discard any that have broken shells, or have their shells open. Place the mussels in a sink or large bowl of cold water. With a sharp knife remove the beard and any bits adhering to the shell. Scrub the shells and wash in several changes of water until the washing water comes out free of grit.

In a large pan melt the butter and sauté the onion, celery leaves and parsley. Cook gently for a few minutes before adding the wine and pepper. Add the mussels, cover the pan and simmer until the shells open (about 6–8 minutes). Transfer the mussels to a warm serving dish and pour over the strained stock. Sprinkle with a little chopped parsley and serve.

LEVER MET PRUINEN

LIVER WITH PRUNES

250 g pitted prunes
1 tablespoon sugar
piece lemon rind
2 tablespoons butter
1 onion, peeled and sliced
625 g calves liver, thinly sliced
1 tablespoon plain flour
1 cup stock (beef or chicken)
2 tablespoons vinegar
salt and freshly ground black pepper
sprig thyme or ½ teaspoon dried thyme
1 bay leaf

Serves 4

Soak the prunes for 2 hours and then drain and place in a small pan. Cover with fresh water, add the sugar and lemon rind and simmer until tender.

Heat the butter in a large pan and sauté the onion until soft. Add the liver and brown lightly on both sides. Remove the liver to a plate, sprinkle flour into the pan and stir, scraping up all the particles clinging to the pan. Add the stock and stir until boiling. Return the liver to the pan and add the drained prunes, vinegar, seasoning and herbs. Cover and simmer for 15 minutes. Serve at once.

ROGNONS DE VEAU À LA LIÉGEOISE

KIDNEYS WITH
JUNIPER BERRIES

4 veal kidneys
butter
4 dessertspoons juniper berries, crushed
freshly ground black pepper
2 tablespoons gin
1 cup jellied stock (veal is best)*
chopped parsley for garnishing

Serves 4

* Jellied veal stock can be made by covering some veal bones in a pan with cold water, adding a bouquet garni and an onion stuck with a couple of cloves and simmering over a gentle heat for about 1½ hours. It can also be made by using a stock cube and powdered gelatine dissolved in a cup of water.

Split the kidneys and remove the cores. Put a dot of butter on top of each kidney and top with a dessertspoon of the crushed juniper berries. Season with pepper. Place the kidneys in a pan and flambé with the gin, add the stock and cook until the kidneys are tender. Remove them to a plate and keep warm while stirring the juices in the pan to amalgamate them. Pour the juices over the kidneys and garnish with chopped parsley.

PURÉE DE CHOUX DE BRUXELLES AUX CHÂTAIGNE

500 g chestnuts
500 g Brussels sprouts
2–3 cups chicken stock
salt and freshly ground black pepper
freshly grated nutmeg

Serves 4

Peel and cook the chestnuts until tender (see page 40). Trim the sprouts and place in a pan, cover with the stock and cook until tender. Season with salt and pepper and drain off any excess stock. Mash the sprouts with a fork until they form a purée. Break the chestnuts into small pieces and fold into the purée (do not mash them). Grate some fresh nutmeg over the dish and serve at once.

VLAAMSE RODEKOOL

1 small red cabbage, shredded (with the core removed)
2 tablespoons vinegar
2 tablespoons port
2 tablespoons butter
1 onion, peeled and sliced into rings
2 cooking apples, peeled, cored and sliced
1 tablespoon brown sugar
bouquet of herbs including parsley, thyme, 1 bay leaf and a slice of lemon rind
salt and freshly ground black pepper
$\frac{1}{2}$ cup water

Serves 4–6

Place the cabbage and vinegar in a bowl and leave to stand for 30 minutes. Put all the ingredients in a large earthenware casserole, cover and cook in a moderate oven for 2–2$\frac{1}{2}$ hours, or until the cabbage is done. Remove the bouquet of herbs and serve.

GÂTEAU ARDENNAIS

250 g potatoes, peeled and cooked until tender
3 egg yolks
3 tablespoons rice flour
1 cup icing sugar
3 egg whites

Serves 4

Preheat the oven to 200°C/400°F.
Mash the cooked potatoes, mix in the egg yolks, rice flour and icing sugar and blend until smooth. Whisk the egg whites until stiff and fold them gently into the potato mixture. Butter an oven tray and arrange the potato mixture on it in a cone shape. Bake in the oven for an hour. This dish is usually served cool with apple sauce.

HAZELNOOTTAART

HAZELNUT CAKE

---

4 egg yolks
$\frac{3}{4}$ cup sugar
1$\frac{1}{2}$ cups ground hazlenuts
1 cup self-raising flour, sifted
4 egg whites
$\frac{1}{2}$ cup hazlenuts for decoration

Icing
$\frac{2}{3}$ cup icing sugar
$\frac{1}{2}$ teaspoon vanilla
water

Serves 6–8

Preheat the oven to 180°C/350°F and grease and dust with flour a 20-cm cake tin.

Beat the egg yolks with $\frac{1}{2}$ cup of the sugar until thick and creamy. Add the ground hazelnuts and gently fold in the sifted flour. Whisk the egg whites until they stand in peaks, fold in the remaining sugar and beat until stiff. Fold the beaten whites into the batter, one-third at a time. The mixture will be quite stiff. Place the mixture in the prepared tin and bake for 45 minutes. Check with a skewer to see if the cake is ready. Allow the cake to cool for 5 minutes before removing it from the cake tin and placing it on a wire rack to cool.

Mix the icing sugar with the vanilla and enough water to make the icing the right consistency. Ice the cake and decorate with hazlenuts.

TARTE AUX FRAMBOISES

RASPBERRY TART

---

225 g butter
50 g castor sugar
1 egg, beaten
2 tablespoons oil
1 teaspoon vanilla essence
1 teaspoon almond essence
500 g plain flour
1 teaspoon baking powder
1 cup raspberry jam
icing sugar for decoration

Serves 4–6

Preheat the oven to 150°C/300°F and grease a 20-cm tin.

Beat the butter and sugar until light and fluffy. Add the beaten egg, then the oil, vanilla and almond essence. Continue to beat until well mixed. Sift in the flour and baking powder and stir. Knead the dough until it has the consistency of crumbly pastry. Roll into a firm ball and leave to stand in the refrigerator for about an hour (or until the dough is firm).

Coarsely grate the dough and place half of it in the bottom of the prepared pan. Slightly warm the jam to a runny consistency and pour over the dough. Top with the rest of the grated dough and bake for 1$\frac{1}{4}$ hours. Dust with icing sugar while still warm. Serve cold.

BELGIUM: Moules à la Bruxelloise. See page 14.

Visiting Burma is like stepping back into another age, a part of its charm being that it is still largely untouched by the Western life-style.

Food in Burma is traditionally eaten with the fingers from a small bowl. The heart of the Burmese meal is rice. This will be accompanied by a selection of other dishes including at least one curry, usually fish or chicken, and assorted sauces, together with salads and raw vegetables. Some of the sauces have strong, sharp tastes and should be taken in small quantities at first. Burmese curries have as their base a paste made up of pounded onions, ginger, chillies, garlic and turmeric. Ngapi, a paste made from dried salted prawns, is also widely used in many dishes.

The Burmese are a most hospitable people and they will often serve an array of 'special guest' food to their visitors. This can contain some surprises such as stewed tea leaves with fried garlic and crunchy grasshoppers. Burmese consider the appearance of a meal almost as important as the flavour and fresh flowers are used both to decorate the table and garnish the food.

AUSTRIA: Kasseler mit Tomatensosse. See page 10.

MOHINGA

FISH SOUP

Fish (mainly fresh water) plays an important part in the Burmese diet. The Irrawaddy River, which runs almost the entire length of the country, is one of several major rivers. The picturesque Inle Lake in the Shan state is famous for the way the fishing boats are manoeuvred along by the boat man standing at the stern on one leg, the other leg being wrapped around the oar.

500 g mackerel (or other fish of your choice), complete with heads
2 tablespoons soy sauce
freshly ground black pepper
6 cups water
1 onion, peeled
salt and pepper
3 tablespoons rice
½ cup finely shredded white cabbage
1 stick celery, finely chopped
1 teaspoon fish sauce (available from Asian food stores)

Serves 4

Ask the fishmonger to clean and fillet the fish for you, reserving the heads. Cut the fillets into small pieces, place in a bowl and sprinkle with the soy sauce and pepper. Make sure that all the pieces are well covered with the liquid.

Put the fish heads into a pan and cover with the water. Add the onion, season with salt and pepper and bring to the boil. Reduce the heat and simmer gently for 45 minutes. Strain into another pan and bring to the boil again. Cook the rice in this stock for 10 minutes. Add the fish, along with its marinade, and simmer gently for 10 minutes. Put in the chopped vegetables and cook until they are just tender. Add the fish sauce, adjust the seasoning and serve.

NHA PE GAW

FISH PATTIES

½ cup oil
2 onions, peeled and chopped
1 clove garlic, peeled and crushed
½ teaspoon chilli powder
¼ teaspoon turmeric
rind of 1 small lemon, finely grated
1 kg raw fish fillets
salt
plain flour
400 g canned tomatoes

Serves 4–6

Heat half the oil in a pan and sauté the onions and the garlic until soft. Add the chilli, turmeric and lemon rind and cook for another 5 minutes, stirring occasionally. Take off the heat, remove half the mixture from the pan and reserve it.

Mince the fish fillets, season to taste with salt and add the reserved onion mixture. Mix well. Take a dessertspoon of the mixture at a time and form into small patties, dust lightly with flour and allow to stand in the refrigerator for ½ an hour.

In a clean pan heat the remaining oil and cook the patties, turning to brown on both sides. Remove when cooked and keep warm. Add the tomatoes to the onion mixture remaining in the first pan, stir and if necessary adjust the seasoning. Return the patties to this pan, cover and simmer gently for 15 minutes. Serve.

OH-NO KHAUKSWE

CHICKEN WITH SAFFRON AND COCONUT MILK

1 large fresh chicken, cut into four pieces
1½ teaspoons powdered saffron
boiling water
2 onions, peeled and chopped
3 cloves garlic, peeled and crushed
1 small piece fresh ginger, peeled and finely chopped

Rub the chicken with the saffron. Place in a pan and cover with boiling water. Cook over a gentle heat until tender (about an hour). Allow to cool slightly, then remove the meat from the bones. Return the bones to the stock, cover and simmer until the stock has reduced by one-third.

Pound the chopped onions, garlic and ginger until smooth (or place in a blender).

Heat the two oils in a heavy based casserole and sauté the sliced onion until brown. Dip the chicken pieces into the puréed onion mixture and

4 tablespoons vegetable oil
2 tablespoons sesame oil
2 extra onions, peeled and sliced
1½ tablespoons powdered lentils
2 cups coconut milk (see page 59)

Serving Suggestions
boiled noodles
**2 eggs, hardboiled, shelled and
  chopped**
**1 small bunch spring onions, trimmed
  and chopped**
1 fresh lime or lemon, cut into wedges
chopped fresh chillies (optional)

Serves 4

add to the sliced onion in the casserole and brown. Strain the stock over the chicken and simmer gently for 15 minutes.

Mix the powdered lentils with a little water to make a thin paste and stir into the casserole. Simmer for another 10 minutes. Add the coconut milk and stir over a gentle heat until it has been absorbed. Adjust the seasoning.

Place the cooked noodles on a serving dish and ladle the chicken over them. Serve garnished with the eggs, spring onions and lime. Serve the chillies in a separate bowl. This Burmese national dish is milder than many of the other traditional Burmese recipes.

A MAIR HNUT   BEEF CURRY

This dish has to stand overnight before cooking. Anchovy essence may be used as a substitute for the ngapi.

4 onions, peeled and pounded to a pulp
1 teaspoon ground ginger
½ teaspoon turmeric
¼ teaspoon chilli powder
1 clove garlic, peeled and crushed
½ teaspoon ngapi (prawn paste)
1 kg lean beef, cut into bite-sized
  pieces
¾ cup natural yoghurt
1 cup oil
½ cup water

Serves 4

Put the pounded onions into a pan with a heavy base and add the ginger, turmeric, chilli powder and garlic. Stir and add the prawn paste and the chopped beef. Lastly stir in the yoghurt and oil and allow to stand overnight.

Next day add ½ cup of water and stir. Bring the curry to the boil, turn the heat right down and simmer gently until the meat is tender. The oil will rise to the surface. During cooking check to see that the liquid has not evaporated and add more water if necessary.

KALA HIN   VEGETABLE CURRY

1.5 kg mixed vegetables (e.g.
  cauliflower, potatoes, zucchini,
  beans)
3 onions, peeled and sliced
½ cup oil
1 teaspoon ginger
½ teaspoon turmeric
1 clove garlic, peeled and crushed
¼ teaspoon chilli powder
salt
water
juice of 1 lemon

Serves 4

Clean the vegetables and cut into pieces of a uniform size. Mix the sliced onions with the oil, ginger, turmeric, garlic and chilli. Add salt to taste. Fry over a high heat for 5 minutes, stirring so the mixture does not burn. Add the vegetables and enough water to just cover them. Simmer until the vegetables are cooked. Squeeze the lemon juice over the curry and serve.

HING NU NWE

SPINACH WITH ONION AND SPICES

1 kg spinach
3 tablespoons oil
1 onion, peeled and sliced
2 cloves garlic, peeled and crushed
½ teaspoon salt
¼ teaspoon chilli powder
¼ teaspoon powdered saffron
½ teaspoon ngapi (prawn paste)*

Serves 4

* Anchovy essence can be substituted.

Wash the spinach thoroughly and shred. Heat the oil and sauté the onion and garlic until soft. Put in the salt, spices and ngapi and stir while cooking for a further 5 minutes. Add the spinach—there should be sufficient water clinging to it to provide enough moisture. Cover and simmer over a gentle heat for 5 minutes. The liquid should have all evaporated when the cooking is completed.

OHN HTAMIN

RICE COOKED WITH COCONUT MILK

Rice is the staple diet of the Burmese. This dish would be served accompanied by a selection of side dishes including a curry, fish, salads and pickles.

4 tablespoons ghee or butter
1 onion, peeled and chopped
250 g rice
3 cups coconut milk (see page 59)
sugar
salt

Serves 4

Melt the ghee in a pan and sauté the onion. Add the rice and cook, stirring until the grains become coated with the ghee. Add the coconut milk, sprinkle with a little sugar and season with salt. Bring to the boil, reduce the heat and simmer gently until the rice is cooked and the coconut milk is absorbed (25–30 minutes).

KHAYAN-CHINDI-JAW

TOMATO RELISH

2 tablespoons oil
2 onions, peeled and sliced
4 cloves garlic, peeled and crushed
750 g tomatoes, peeled and chopped
1 teaspoon turmeric
4 teaspoons dried prawns, ground
½ teaspoon sugar

Heat the oil in a pan over a medium heat and sauté the onions and garlic until soft. Add the tomatoes, turmeric, prawns and sugar. Bring to the boil, cover and simmer for about 10 minutes. Serve cold as an accompaniment to rice and curries.

THANHAT

CUCUMBER SALAD

3 cups water
¼ cup white vinegar
2 large green cucumbers, peeled, seeded and cut into strips
2 tablespoons sesame seeds
8 cloves garlic, peeled and finely chopped

Place the water and the vinegar in a pan and bring to the boil. Cook the cucumbers in this liquid until they are transparent. Drain and allow to cool.

Heat the sesame seeds in a heavy bottomed pan until they are brown. Remove and allow to cool.

Deep fry the garlic and onion in the oil until golden. Drain and reserve the oil.

1 onion, peeled and finely chopped
¼ cup oil
1 teaspoon turmeric
salt
1 teaspoon sugar

Serves 4–6

Mix the turmeric, salt and sugar and 3 tablespoons of the reserved oil in a bowl and add the cucumber. Mix well. Serve garnished with the garlic, onions and sesame seeds.

GIN THOK   SALAD OF CASHEW NUTS AND GINGER

125 g fresh ginger, peeled and shredded
salt
juice of 2 limes or 1½ lemons
¾ cup sesame seeds
pinch of sugar
¾ cup cashew nuts

Serves 4

Place the ginger in a bowl, sprinkle with salt and leave to stand for 15 minutes. Rinse in a fine sieve with cold water, squeezing to remove any excess water. Place in a dish and cover with the lime juice. Leave to stand until just before serving.

Place the sesame seeds in a dry pan and cook over a gentle heat until a golden colour.

Drain the liquid from the ginger and sprinkle with a little sugar. Arrange the ginger, sesame seeds and cashews in separate groups on a small platter and serve.

SANWIN MAKIN   SEMOLINA CAKE

185 g fine semolina
2½ cups milk
2 cups coconut milk (see page 59)
2 eggs
250 g castor sugar
2 ground black cardamom seeds
50 g slivered almonds
1 tablespoon toasted white sesame
    seeds

Serves 6–8

Preheat the oven to 180°C/350°F and grease a 25-cm cake tin.

Put the semolina in a heavy based pan and cook over a gentle heat until golden, stirring to prevent it from burning. Allow to cool. Heat the milk and coconut milk in another pan. Pour the heated milk onto the semolina and stir over a gentle heat until it becomes very thick.

Beat the eggs and sugar until light and frothy and fold in the ground cardamom and almonds. Add this to the semolina and stir until thoroughly mixed. Pour into the prepared tin, smooth the top and sprinkle with sesame seeds. Stand the tin in a baking dish containing about 3 cm of cold water. Cook in the oven for approximately 2½ hours. Although the cake will be firm on the outside, the inside will remain very moist. If the top becomes too brown during cooking, cover the cake with foil and continue baking. Allow to cool in the tin. In Burma this cake is cut into diamond shapes for serving.

CHOW-CHAW   ROSE WATER JELLY

Agar-agar is made from seaweed and has setting properties that do not need refrigeration. It sets to a solid texture and when cut into pieces will hold its shape.

2¾ cups water
3 teaspoons agar-agar powder
¾ cup sugar
100 g creamed coconut
few drops red food colouring
1 tablespoon rose water

Serves 6

Place the water and the agar-agar in a pan and stir over a gentle heat until the powder has dissolved. Simmer for 1 minute, stirring to distribute the agar-agar evenly through the liquid. Add the sugar and creamed coconut and cook, stirring until they have dissolved. Remove from the heat and add a few drops of food colouring and the rose water. Stir.

Rinse a bowl with cold water and pour the jelly into it and allow to set. Cut the jelly into triangular shapes and serve on its own or with a platter of fresh fruit.

The Chinese, along with the French and Italians, can claim to have made the greatest contribution to the world's cuisine. The range of Chinese food is enormous and it seems that almost anything can be cooked and made enjoyable, including the feet of birds, snakes and even mice!

Chinese food combines colour, flavour, aroma and texture. Preparation is all important and more time is spent preparing food than in cooking it. Ingredients are usually cut into pieces of about the same size, both to give an appearance of approximate uniformity and to equalise cooking time. A sharp cleaver and a chopping block are of great help in preparation. The wok is the most commonly used cooking utensil although a bamboo steamer is also useful. Chinese food is usually eaten from small bowls using chopsticks.

China is a vast country and the variation in food between regions is considerable. However, the best known Chinese food styles can be divided into four main types. Cantonese food is often steamed or par-boiled before being lightly fried. Rice is always served with a Cantonese meal. Pekingese food tends to be fairly substantial, wine and spices are commonly used and dishes often have a crispy texture as in the famous Peking Duck. The food of Shanghai is cooked longer and more slowly and contains more starch; oil is used liberally and rice is often replaced by noodles. Garlic and ginger are used for flavouring. The main characteristic of Szechuan food is that it is highly spiced.

The Chinese meal has a number of other features that differentiate it from those of the West. Soups, for example, do not come at the beginning of the meal but are served with it or at the end. Tea, either the green or red (black) variety, is drunk throughout the day and is consumed without milk or sugar from small porcelain cups.

TAN HUA TANG

8 cups stock (fish or chicken)
3 tablespoons parsley, finely chopped
¼ cup chives, chopped
¼ cup spring onions, chopped
6 small tomatoes, skinned and chopped
salt and freshly ground black pepper
½ teaspoon monosodium glutamate
2 eggs

Serves 6

Bring the stock to the boil and add the parsley, chives, spring onions and tomatoes. Season to taste and sprinkle in the monosodium glutamate. Whisk the eggs and spoon equal quantities into each soup plate. Ladle in the boiling soup. This will cook the egg. Serve at once.

MUI TSE PAI GWAT

1½ tablespoons fermented, salted black beans (available in cans from Asian food stores)
3 tablespoons vegetable oil
1 piece fresh ginger (about 4 cm long), peeled and chopped
1 kg pork spare ribs, cut into 5-cm pieces
1 teaspoon salt
500 g plums, seeded, peeled and chopped

Sauce
3 teaspoons sugar
3 tablespoons soy sauce
3 tablespoons sherry
1 tablespoon cornflour

Serves 4–6

Soak the black beans in water for 20 minutes and mash them. Heat the oil in a wok or pan and add the beans and the ginger and cook, stirring for 2 minutes. Add the spare ribs, sprinkle with salt and cook until the ribs are browned (5–10 minutes). Place this mixture in a large metal steamer, along with the prepared plums.

Place the sugar, soy sauce, sherry and cornflour into a small bowl and mix until smooth. Pour this sauce over the spare ribs and plums in the steamer and stir until all ingredients are thoroughly mixed. Cover and steam for about 45 minutes, or until the spare ribs are tender.

MA-P'O TOU-FU

6 Chinese mushrooms
3 tablespoons vegetable oil
1 onion, peeled and sliced
2 cloves garlic, peeled and crushed
125 g pork, minced
½ cup beef stock
2 tablespoons sherry
3 tablespoons soy sauce
dash of Tobasco
freshly ground black pepper
250 g bean curd, cut into pieces
1 tablespoon cornflour, mixed to a smooth paste with a little water
sesame oil

Serves 4

Soak the mushrooms in hot water until plump and then slice them. Heat the oil in a wok or large pan and stir-fry the onion and garlic for 3 minutes. Add the sliced mushrooms and meat and cook for another 3 minutes. While still over the heat stir in the stock, sherry, soy sauce and Tobasco until well mixed. Season with pepper, add the bean curd and stir to distribute evenly. Over a low heat blend in the cornflour paste, stirring until the sauce thickens. Sprinkle with sesame oil and serve.

DAAN GUEN

Pancakes
2 eggs
1 tablespoon cornflour
oil for frying
1 tablespoon plain flour
water

Filling
100 g pork, finely minced
1 spring onion, chopped
½ teaspoon fresh ginger, finely chopped
2 teaspoons Chinese rice wine or sherry
1½ teaspoons cornflour
salt
6 dried Chinese mushroms, soaked until plump
100 g bean shoots

Sauce
1 tablespoon Chinese rice wine
2 tablespoons soy sauce
freshly grated ginger

Serves 4

To make the egg pancakes, beat the eggs with the cornflour. Heat a little oil in a wok or frying pan and tilt it to make sure the surface is well coated. Pour in half the egg mixture and swirl around until there is a thin coating over the pan. Turn to cook both sides. When cooked, carefully lift the pancake onto a flat plate and repeat with the rest of the mixture. Put the flour in a bowl and add a little water to form a thin paste. Lightly brush the surface of the pancakes with this liquid.

To make the filling, mix together the pork, spring onion, ginger, rice wine and cornflour and season with salt. Divide this mixture and place half on each pancake. Chop the mushrooms and divide them between the pancakes, along with the bean shoots. Fold the pancakes up into packages and seal the edges with a little more of the flour and water paste. Press the edges together firmly.

To make the sauce, combine the rice wine, soy sauce, a little ginger and mix well.

Heat some oil in a large pan, carefully lower the rolls into the pan and cook for a few minutes. Increase the heat and cook for a further 10 minutes, or until golden. Drain and serve with the sauce.

M HEUNG NAU

1 fresh duck (2–2½ kg), cut into four pieces
boiling water
2 pieces fresh ginger (about 2 cm long), peeled
6 spring onions, cleaned
4 tablespoons soy sauce
4 tablespoons rice wine or sherry
2 heaped tablespoons sugar
1 teaspoon five-spice powder
8 Chinese dried mushrooms, soaked until plump
1 large carrot, scraped and sliced
500 g Chinese cabbage, cut into large chunks

Serves 4

Put the duck pieces in a large pan and cover with boiling water. Place over a high heat and bring the water back to the boil. Boil for 5 minutes. Strain off two-thirds of the water and add the ginger, onions, soy sauce, rice wine, sugar and five-spice powder. Return to the boil and cover with a tight fitting lid. Simmer gently for an hour. Add the mushrooms, carrot and cabbage and simmer for another ½ hour. Serve with rice or noodles.

CHENG JU NAU YOOK

BEEF WITH GREEN PEPPERS

4 tablespoons cooking oil
2 cloves garlic, peeled and crushed
1 piece fresh ginger (about 4 cm long),
    peeled and finely grated
500 g rump steak, sliced into fine, short
    strips
salt and pepper
2 green peppers, seeded and cut into
    strips
1 teaspoon sugar
4 tablespoons soy sauce
2 tomatoes, peeled and quartered
3 tablespoons cornflour, mixed to a
    paste with a little cold water
4 spring onions, chopped

Serves 4

Heat the oil in a wok or pan and fry the garlic and ginger for a few seconds. Add the sliced beef, season with salt and pepper and stir-fry until the beef is browned—about 2 minutes. Add the green peppers, sugar and soy sauce, cover the pan and cook gently for 5 minutes. Add the tomatoes and cornflour paste and stir until the sauce thickens. Serve garnished with chopped spring onions.

GWOO LO YOOK

SWEET AND SOUR PORK

60 g plain flour
90 g cornflour
1 teaspoon salt
1 egg yolk
3 tablespoons cold water
1 egg white
oil for frying
500 g pork fillets, cut into cubes

Sauce
2 tablespoons sugar
2 tablespoons soy sauce
2 tablespoons wine vinegar
1 tablespoon Chinese rice wine or
    sherry
oil
1 onion, peeled and cut into eighths
1 red or green pepper, seeded and
    chopped
1 large carrot, scraped and sliced into
    lengths about 3 cm long
1 clove garlic, peeled and crushed
1 small piece fresh ginger, peeled and
    finely chopped
1 tablespoon cornflour, mixed to a
    smooth paste with a little water

Serves 4

Sift the flour, cornflour and salt into a bowl, make a well in the centre and add the egg yolk and the cold water. Mix until the batter is smooth, adding more water if necessary. Whisk the egg white until stiff and fold into the batter.

Heat some oil in a pan (about 4 cm deep) and when very hot dip the pieces of pork into the batter and cook, a few pieces at a time, until golden. Remove and drain on absorbent paper. Repeat until all the pork has been cooked. Keep warm while preparing the sauce.

To make the sauce, mix together the sugar, soy sauce, wine vinegar and rice wine in a small bowl. Heat a little oil in a wok and stir-fry the onion, pepper and carrot for a couple of minutes. Add the garlic, ginger and the soy sauce mixture from the bowl. Bring to the boil and simmer for a minute. Add the cornflour paste and stir until boiling. The mixture will thicken and become clear. Take care not to cook for too long as the vegetables should retain their crispness.

Arrange the pieces of pork on a serving dish, cover with the sauce and serve at once.

GWOO LO YOUYU

500 g fresh squid, with the head and
    tentacles removed
1 tablespoon cornflour
pinch of salt
2 tablespoons Chinese rice wine
3 tablespoons vegetable oil
2 cloves garlic, peeled and crushed
piece fresh ginger (about 2 cm long),
    peeled and finely chopped
1 onion, peeled and sliced
1 small green pepper, seeded and
    chopped
100 g snow peas, topped and tailed with
    the strings removed if necessary
2 tablespoons sliced water chestnuts

Sauce
3 tablespoons soy sauce
2 tablespoons sugar
2 tablespoons vinegar
2 tablespoons Chinese rice wine
1 heaped teaspoon cornflour
1 tablespoon sesame oil
2 tablespoons vegetable oil

Serves 4

Cut each squid open so that it becomes a flat piece. Remove the transparent membrane. Rinse in cold running water and cut into strips about 5 cm long. Combine the cornflour, salt and rice wine and mix until smooth. Marinate the squid in this mixture while preparing the other ingredients.

To prepare the sauce, place the soy sauce, sugar, vinegar, rice wine, cornflour, sesame oil and vegetable oil in a bowl and stir until well mixed.

Heat half the 3 tablespoons of oil in a wok, add the squid with the garlic and ginger and stir-fry for 2 minutes (do not cook for too long or the squid will become tough). Remove and keep warm. Add the rest of the oil and cook the onion and green pepper until they are just softening. Add the snow peas and water chestnuts and stir-fry for just a minute. Add the squid and sauce and cook, stirring until mixed. Serve at once.

CHOW FAN

This is an elegant version of fried rice and makes an excellent accompaniment to many Chinese dishes.

250 g shrimps, peeled and de-veined
1 tablespoon rice wine
½ teaspoon salt
8 dried Chinese mushrooms
6 tablespoons vegetable oil
2 eggs, beaten with 1 tablespoon water
    and pinch of salt
4 spring onions, including tops,
    chopped
250 g ham, diced
125 g roast pork, diced
½ cup bamboo shoots, diced
200 g cooked green peas
6 water chestnuts, diced
5 cups cooked white rice
salt and pepper

Serves 6

Marinate the shrimps in the rice wine and salt for about 1 hour. Soak the mushrooms in hot water until plump and then remove and slice them.

Heat 1 tablespoon of the oil in a wok, pour in the whisked eggs and cook until set. Remove from the pan, dice and reserve. Add the rest of the oil to the pan and stir-fry the shrimps, spring onions, ham, pork, bamboo shoots, peas, water chestnuts and mushrooms for 2 minutes. Add the cooked rice, season with salt and pepper and mix in the diced eggs. Stir to ensure that the ingredients are evenly distributed.

It is possible to prepare this dish in advance. Simply re-heat by stir-frying before serving.

WONG NA BA

1½ cups chestnuts
6 dried Chinese mushrooms
500 g Chinese cabbage
2 tablespoons vegetable oil
2 tablespoons lard
2 tablespoons dried prawns
piece fresh ginger (about 3 cm long),
    peeled and finely chopped
1 cup chicken stock
3 tablespoons sherry
3 tablespoons soy sauce
1 tablespoon sugar

Serves 4

Boil the chestnuts for about an hour, drain and shell. Soak the mushrooms in hot water until plump and then slice them. Clean the cabbage and cut the leaves into pieces.

Heat the oil and lard in a wok or large pan and sauté the prawns, chestnuts, mushrooms and ginger and stir-fry for 3 minutes. Add the cabbage and cook, stirring until mixed. Pour in the stock, sherry and soy sauce and sprinkle the mixture with the sugar. Cook over a gentle heat for 15–20 minutes, stirring from time to time. Serve.

DUNG GU CHOW CHENG DOW

12 dried Chinese mushrooms
500 g snow peas
2 tablespoons oil
1 clove garlic, peeled and crushed
1 tablespoon soy sauce
½ teaspoon sugar
½ teaspoon salt

Serves 4–6

Soak the mushrooms in warm water. When they are plump, slice the caps. Cut the tips from the snow peas and string them if necessary.

Heat the oil in a wok, add the garlic and the mushrooms and cook, stirring for a couple of minutes. Add the snow peas, soy sauce, sugar and salt. Stir over the heat for several minutes and serve at once. The snow peas should remain crisp.

CHA-YEH-TAN

This is a national dish, but each region has its own variations. It can be served as a snack or as an accompaniment to a main meal.

6 eggs
water
2 teaspoons salt
2 whole star anise
3 tablespoons soy sauce
2–3 teaspoons black tea leaves

Serves 4–6

Hardboil the eggs for 10–15 minutes. Remove from the water and run under cold water. When cool, tap the eggs gently with a heavy spoon all over the surface to create a network of very fine cracks. Put the eggs back into the pot and cover with fresh water. Add salt, star anise, soy sauce and tea leaves. Bring to the boil and simmer for 45 minutes to an hour. Make sure that the eggs are covered with water throughout this time. Allow to cool in the water. When cool peel the shells off and you will have beautiful eggs covered in a marbled pattern.

LIANG-PAN-HUANG-KUA

CHINESE CUCUMBER SALAD

1 large continental cucumber

Dressing
1 tablespoon wine vinegar
1½ teaspoons soy sauce
2 teaspoons sesame oil
good pinch of chilli powder
2 teaspoons sugar
½ teaspoon salt

Serves 4–6

Peel and remove the seeds from the cucumber and cut it into slices. Place in a serving bowl. To make the dressing, mix all the ingredients together well. Pour over the cucumber and chill before serving.

JAR WONTON

DEEP FRIED SWEET DUMPLINGS

Wonton wrappers are available from stores stocking Asian provisions and some super-markets. However, for those with the time or the inclination they can be made at home without too much difficulty.

Wrappers
1 egg, beaten
¼ cup cold water
250 g plain flour, sifted
pinch of salt
oil for frying
icing sugar for decoration

Makes about 24 wrappers

Filling
375 g Chinese dates, finely chopped
125 g walnuts, finely chopped
1 teaspoon orange rind, finely grated
1½ tablespoons fresh orange juice

To make the wrappers, mix the beaten egg with the cold water. Place the sifted flour and salt in a bowl and make a well in the centre. Add the egg and water mixture, working it into the flour until a soft dough forms. Knead the dough lightly on a floured surface. Divide the mixture in two and leave one half covered with a damp cloth. On a lightly floured surface roll out the dough to the thickness of heavy paper. Cut the dough into 7-cm squares and stack between sheets of waxed paper. Repeat with the remaining dough.

To make the filling, combine the dates, walnuts and orange rind. Moisten with the orange juice and stir until the mixture clings together. Add more juice if necessary.

Place a heaped teaspoon of the filling diagonally across the centre of a wonton wrapper. Roll up like a parcel, making sure all the filling is enclosed. With dampened fingers seal the edges so that none of the filling escapes during cooking. (As an alternative you may place the mixture in the centre of the wrapper, roll the wrapper around the filling and twist the edges together, like a bon-bon.) Repeat until all the filling is used.

Heat enough oil to deep fry the wontons. When the liquid is smoking, gently lower the wontons, a few at a time, into the oil and cook until golden. Drain, dust with icing sugar and serve.

When Catherine de Medici left Florence in 1533 to marry the heir to the throne of France, she took along her Florentine cooks and a collection of kitchen utensils and cutlery, including the fork, hitherto unknown to the French. As well as improving local table manners and passing on their culinary skills, the Florentines introduced new vegetables into France and aroused in the French an interest in fine cuisine which has never waned.

The gastronomes of France have been especially blessed. The Mediterranean and Atlantic produce superb seafood; lush pastures provide well-fed cattle and excellent dairy products while great wines have been made in France since Roman times. These factors, combined with a national character which regards cooking and eating as an art form, make French food, in the opinion of many, simply the best in the world.

While the French employ energy and imagination in the preparation of their food, it is in marketing that their secret lies. Nothing but the best will do and it is interesting to observe the French inspecting the produce displayed in the markets before making their choice.

Sauces play an important part in French cooking and a stock pot is usually on hand to assist in the making of these and to prepare soups and stews. Fresh herbs are used to impart their own special flavours including the frequently used bouquet garni, a muslin bag containing bay leaves, parsley and thyme. The French use vegetables that are young and tender and full of flavour. Wine and olive oil are widely used. Simplicity is valued too and some of the very best French dishes are slow-cooking composites of peasant origin.

POTAGE BONNE FEMME

POTATO SOUP

This soup is simple to prepare, is economical to make and has a fresh, sweet taste.

3 tablespoons butter
2 large leeks, washed and chopped, or 2
   large onions, peeled and sliced
250 g carrots, scraped and chopped
500 g potatoes, peeled and chopped
1 litre water or light stock
1 teaspoon sugar
salt and freshly ground black pepper
½ cup cream
finely chopped parsley

Serves 4–6

Melt the butter in a heavy based pan and add the leeks and the carrots. Cover and cook over a gentle heat to allow the vegetables to absorb the butter. Add the potatoes, the water and sugar and season with salt and pepper. Bring to the boil and simmer for ½ an hour. Purée the soup and adjust the seasoning. Place the soup in a tureen, pour in a little of the cream and sprinkle with the parsley. Serve the remaining cream at the table.

GOUGÈRE

CHOUX PASTRY PUFF FLAVOURED WITH CHEESE

These puffs are excellent served as a snack with a glass of red wine, or in winter they make a good accompaniment to a bowl of soup.

1¼ cups milk
60 g butter
½ teaspoon salt
pepper
125 g plain flour
4 eggs
90 g Gruyère cheese, grated

Serves 4–6

Preheat the oven to 200°C/400°F.

Bring the milk to the boil and allow to cool. Strain. Cut the butter into small pieces, add to the milk with the salt and a little pepper. Return to the heat and rapidly bring to the boil. The butter and milk should amalgamate.

Sift the flour and add it all at once to the milk and butter mixture. Over a gentle heat stir with a wooden spoon until a smooth, thick paste forms. It will come away from the sides of the pan. Remove from the heat and add the eggs, one at a time, stirring each one in thoroughly before adding the next. When all the eggs are added the paste should be shiny and smooth. Stir in the grated cheese, reserving a little for garnishing.

Place a piece of foil on a baking tray or sheet and mark out a circle about 20 cm in diameter (a plate can be used for this—trace around the outside of it). Take about 1 tablespoon of the mixture at a time and position around the circle. Add a second layer on top of the first, spoonful by spoonful, and smooth out with a palette-knife when finished. There should be a small well left in the centre. Brush the top with a little milk and sprinkle with the reserved cheese.

Cook in the preheated oven for about 45 minutes. Do not open the oven during cooking or the gougère will collapse. To test press lightly—the pastry should be firm. If you wish to serve the gougère warm, turn the oven off and leave the puff to stand in the warm oven for 5 minutes before serving. Cut into chunks and serve.

OEUFS EN COCOTTE À L'OSEILLE

EGGS WITH SORREL

Sorrel grows in clumps rather like spinach. It has a slightly acidic taste and is reputed to be good for the blood and an aid to digestion. It has a particular affinity to eggs.

Lightly butter four ramekin dishes and preheat the oven to 180°C/350°F.

Wash the sorrel thoroughly, remove the stems and chop the leaves. Melt the butter in a pan (it is best not to use an aluminium pan when cooking sorrel because of its acid content) and add the chopped sorrel leaves. Cook over a gentle heat until soft.

125 g sorrel
2 tablespoons butter
1 cup cream
salt and freshly ground black pepper
4 eggs

Serves 4

Bring the cream to the boil in a small pan. Pour half of the boiled cream on to the sorrel and season to taste. Purée the sorrel mixture and divide it evenly between the four ramekin dishes.

Break an egg into each dish, season lightly and top with the remaining cream. Place the ramekins in a baking tray containing a little boiling water. Cook in a moderate oven for about 10 minutes, or until the eggs are just set. Serve at once.

QUICHE LORRAINE

CHEESE AND BACON FLAN

Shortcrust Pastry
250 g plain flour
pinch of salt
60 g butter
60 g lard
cold water

Filling
2 eggs
1 egg yolk
90 g Gruyère cheese, grated
30 g Parmesan cheese, grated
¾ cup cream
salt and freshly ground black pepper
1 tablespoon butter
125 g rindless bacon, cut into pieces
fresh chives, chopped

Serves 4

Preheat the oven to 200°C/400°F and grease a 20-cm flan tin.

To make the pastry, sift the flour and salt into a bowl and rub in the butter and lard with your fingertips until the mixture resembles fine breadcrumbs. Add about 2 tablespoons of cold water and mix until you have a firm dough. If necessary add a little more water—the pastry should not be too damp. Cover the pastry and stand in the refrigerator for ½ an hour before using.

Line the flan tin with the pastry and cover the base with waxed paper and weigh down with pastry beans. Bake blind for 10 minutes. (This step stops the pastry from becoming soggy.) Allow to cool slightly.

Melt the butter in a small pan and lightly fry the bacon. Sprinkle the bacon pieces in the bottom of the flan case. Beat the eggs and yolk in a bowl. Add the grated cheeses, cream, chives and season with salt and pepper and whisk well to mix. Pour over the bacon pieces in the flan case. Cook for about 30 minutes or until golden and firm.

SALADE NIÇOISE

MIXED SALAD WITH TUNA AND OLIVES

5 tomatoes
1 medium onion
1 green pepper
10 small radishes
4 stalks celery
2 hardboiled eggs
170 g canned tuna
12 black olives
8 anchovy fillets

French Dressing
1 cup olive oil or other salad oil
⅓ cup wine vinegar
1 clove garlic, peeled and crushed
½ teaspoon salt
½ teaspoon sugar
½ teaspoon French mustard
freshly gound black pepper

Serves 6–8

In France this salad is usually served as an *hors-d'oeuvre*. However, it makes an excellent lunch when accompanied by crusty French bread and a glass of wine.

Wipe the tomatoes and cut into segments. Peel and slice the onion into rings. Seed the green pepper and slice. Wash and trim the radishes, leaving a little of the green on top. Wash the celery and cut into bite-sized pieces. Peel and quarter the hardboiled eggs. Break the tuna into chunks.

To make the dressing, put all the ingredients into a screw-top jar and shake until well mixed. Kept covered in the refrigerator, it can be stored until needed.

Place all the salad ingredients into a large bowl, dress and toss lightly.

BOURRIDE

Bourride has its origins in Provence. It is best made with two or three different kinds of fish, but it is perfectly acceptable to use just one type, for example, bream. The accompanying sauce, an aïoli, is a garlic flavoured mayonnaise.

1 kg fresh fish
2 slices French bread per person,
  toasted

Aïoli   (Garlic Mayonnaise)
3 cloves garlic, peeled and crushed
2 egg yolks
pinch of dry mustard
1 cup olive oil
juice of ½ lemon
salt and freshly ground black pepper

Court Bouillon   (Fish Stock)
fish heads (reserved when cleaning the
  fish)
1 litre cold water
1 wineglass white wine
2 tablespoons wine vinegar
1 onion, peeled and stuck with 2 cloves
bouquet garni
piece orange rind
small piece fresh fennel

Serves 4–6

The aïoli is best made in a pestle and mortar. Warm these by running hot water over them for a few minutes, then dry them thoroughly. Place the garlic in the bowl and add the egg yolks, one at a time, and stir until smooth. Blend in the mustard and add the oil, drop by drop at first, stirring constantly. As the aïoli thickens the oil can be added at a faster rate. When the sauce is thick and shiny add the strained lemon juice and season with salt and pepper.

To make the court bouillon, clean the fish and place the heads in a large pan and add the cold water, wine, vinegar, onion (stuck with a couple of cloves), bouquet garni, orange rind and fennel. Bring to the boil and simmer gently for about an hour. Strain and return and stock to the heat and simmer until it reduces by about one-third. Move the pan from the heat and reserve.

Cut the fish into thick slices and poach gently in the court bouillon for about 10 minutes, taking care the pieces do not break up. Remove the fish, drain and keep warm.

Make a sauce by placing half the aïoli into the top of a double boiler and add a cup of strained court bouillon. Stir until the sauce is thick. Do not allow it to boil.

Arrange the fish on a large serving dish with the toasted French bread to one side. Ladle the sauce generously over the fish and serve the remainder of the aïoli in a jug.

RIS DE VEAU   VEAL SWEETBREADS COOKED WITH CREAM AND MUSHROOMS

Sweetbreads have a similar flavour and texture to brains. This dish is very rich and is best served in small portions.

500 g veal sweetbreads
salt
squeeze of lemon juice
125 g butter
4 slices bread, crusts removed
½ small onion, peeled and sliced
185 g mushrooms, wiped with a damp
  cloth and sliced
freshly ground black pepper
½ teaspoon freshly grated nutmeg
¼ cup cream

Serves 4

Soak the sweetbreads in cold water for a few hours and drain. Place them in a pan and cover with fresh water. Add a little salt and lemon juice. Bring to simmering point and cook very gently for about 10 minutes. Drain the sweetbreads and plunge them into cold water. Drain, place on a plate and cover with another plate. Put a weight on top of the plate and leave for an hour or two. This will make the sweetbreads firm and easier to slice. When ready, remove any membrane and cut the sweetbreads into slices.

Melt some of the butter in a pan and sauté the sliced sweetbreads until golden. Remove from the pan and keep warm. Add some more butter and fry the bread on both sides until crisp. Remove and keep warm. Sauté the onion and the mushrooms in the remaining butter and season with salt, pepper and nutmeg. Add the cream and stir to amalgamate. Place the sweetbreads on the crisp bread on warmed plates and spoon on the cream sauce. Serve at once.

FRANCE: Ingredients for Bourride (Fish with Garlic Mayonnaise). See this page.

COQ AU VIN   CHICKEN IN RED WINE SAUCE

This dish is best eaten with boiled potatoes or lightly buttered noodles and a green salad.

90 g butter
16 small pickling onions, peeled
125 g bacon, cut into pieces
250 g button mushrooms, wiped with a
    damp cloth and bases trimmed
1 plump chicken (about 1.5 kg), cut
    into pieces
flour for dusting chicken
bouquet garni
2 cloves garlic, peeled and crushed
½ bottle red wine
salt and freshly ground black pepper
1 tablespoon extra butter
1 tablespoon plain flour
freshly chopped parsley for garnishing

Serves 4

Melt the 90 g of butter in a large casserole with a heavy base. Brown the onions, adding the bacon after about 5 minutes. Cook for a further 2 minutes before adding the mushrooms. Cook for another couple of minutes, taking care not to burn. Remove vegetables and reserve.

Dust the chicken lightly with flour and add to the bacon in the casserole. Sauté until the chicken pieces are golden brown. Return the vegetables to the casserole, add the bouquet garni, garlic and wine and season with salt and pepper. Cover and cook in a moderate oven for about 45 minutes. Remove from the oven and strain off the sauce. Keep the chicken pieces and vegetables warm in the casserole. Reduce the sauce by boiling it rapidly on top of the stove.

Work the extra tablespoon of butter into the tablespoon of flour. Break the mixture into pieces and stir into the sauce. Allow the sauce to come to the boil while stirring. Pour over the chicken and vegetables in the casserole. Return it to the oven and cook for about another ½ hour (pierce the chicken to make sure it is tender). Garnish with finely chopped parsley and serve.

CASSOULET   BAKED HARICOT BEANS AND MEAT

The cassoulet is French country food at its best. The dish originated in the south-west of France, but is now thought of as a national dish. One of the pleasures of the cassoulet is the aroma that permeates the house during the long, slow cooking. It is a heavy dish and usually is best served in cool weather when something warm and nourishing is required.

500 g dried white haricot beans
2 onions, peeled
4 cloves garlic, peeled
bouquet garni
250 g bacon, in one piece
125 g fresh pork rind
250 g coarse garlic sausage (the type
    used for frying or boiling)
½ shoulder of lamb (about 500 g)
500 g belly of pork
½ duck or pieces of goose (if possible)
salt and freshly ground pepper
fresh breadcrumbs

Serves 4–6

Place the beans in a large pan, cover with cold water and allow to soak overnight. Drain, return to the pan and cover with fresh water. Add the onions, garlic, bouquet garni, bacon, pork rind and sausage. Bring to the boil and simmer gently until the beans are almost cooked. Meanwhile roast the lamb and pork, and the duck or goose if it is being used. Allow the meat to cool slightly, remove the bones and cut the meat into pieces.

Take out the meat and pork rind from the pot of beans and cut into pieces. Drain the beans, reserving the liquid. Choose a large heatproof earthenware casserole and place alternate layers of beans and meat in the casserole, seasoning as you go. Half fill the casserole with some of the liquid in which the beans have been cooked. Cover the top with a layer of fresh breadcrumbs and cook in a slow oven (150°C/300°F) until a crust forms. Stir this crust into the casserole and sprinkle the top with more crumbs. Repeat this procedure until a third crust has formed. The cassoulet is now ready to serve. It should be very moist and the beans tender. This dish can be prepared in advance and reheated.

CHINA: Cha-Yeh-Tan (Braised Tea Eggs). See page 27.

FRANCE

BOEUF EN DAUBE À LA PROVENÇAL

BEEF CASSEROLE
FROM PROVENCE

oil for cooking
1.5 kg rump steak, cut into large pieces
250 g bacon, chopped
1 large onion, peeled and sliced
3 cloves garlic, peeled and crushed
¾ cup red wine
small wineglass brandy
¾ cup stock
bouquet garni
piece orange rind
salt and freshly ground black pepper
125 g black olives, stoned

Serves 4–6

Heat the oil in a heavy based pan and add the meat, bacon, onion and garlic. Brown over a rapid heat, stirring from time to time, taking care not to let it burn.

Bring the wine to the boil in a separate pan. Pour the brandy over the meat and set it alight (flambé). Add the heated wine, stock, bouquet garni and orange rind to the meat and season with salt and pepper. Cover and cook in a very slow oven for about 3–3½ hours. When cooked, the meat should be tender enough to cut with a spoon. Skim any fat from the surface, add the olives, and return to the oven for another ½ hour.

If desired, this dish can be prepared in advance and heated up before serving.

RATATOUILLE

RAGOÛT OF VEGETABLES

Ratatouille, a Provençal dish of vegetables, can be eaten by itself, or as an accompaniment to meat, fish or chicken. It is equally good hot or cold.

2 large aubergines
salt
2 large onions
2 red or green pimentos
3–4 large tomatoes
boiling water
olive oil
salt and freshly ground black pepper
2 cloves garlic, crushed (optional)

Serves 4

Wipe the aubergines with a damp cloth and slice into thick round segments. Sprinkle each slice with salt and leave in a colander to drain. This removes the bitter taste. Peel the onions and slice. Wipe and slice the pimentos, taking care to remove the core and all the seeds. Plunge the tomatoes into boiling water for 2–3 minutes to loosen the skins, and then peel them. Rinse the aubergines under running water to remove the salt and pat them dry with absorbent paper.

Heat the oil in a large deep frying pan. Add the onions and garlic and sauté, taking care that they don't burn. Add the pimentos and aubergines and cook gently for 10 minutes. Stir in the tomatoes, cover the pan and simmer gently for 30 minutes. Season with salt and pepper.

OIGNONS À LA MONÉGASQUE

SMALL ONIONS COOKED WITH
PORT AND CURRANTS

This dish can be eaten by itself with crusty fresh bread and butter, or as an accompaniment to cold meat. It will keep for several days if covered and refrigerated.

3 tablespoons olive oil
24 small pickling onions, peeled
1 sherry glass wine vinegar
1 sherry glass port
2 tablespoons brown sugar
½ cup currants
salt and pepper

Serves 4

Warm the oil in a heavy pan and sauté the onions until they start to brown. Add the vinegar, port, brown sugar, currants, salt and pepper and stir carefully with a wooden spoon. Simmer on a low heat until the onions are quite soft and the sauce has thickened.

34

POMMES DE TERRE AU BASILIC

POTATOES COOKED WITH
CREAM AND BASIL

1 kg good potatoes
boiling water
1½ tablespoons butter
1½ tablespoons plain flour
1 cup milk
¾ cup cream
1 tablespoon fresh basil, finely
   chopped, or ½ teaspoon dried basil
2 cloves garlic, peeled and crushed
salt and freshly ground black pepper
fresh parsley or basil, finely chopped
   for garnishing

Serves 4–6

Peel the potatoes and slice to a uniform thickness. Bring a large pan of water to the boil, add the potatoes, bring the water to the boil again and simmer for 2 minutes. Drain. This procedure will stop the sauce from curdling.

Melt the butter and mix in the flour. Stir this mixture over heat for 2 minutes, taking care not to let it burn. Remove from the heat and stir in the milk, cream, basil and garlic and season with salt and pepper. Return the pan to the heat and stir until the sauce boils. Carefully fold in the potatoes, which should be just covered by the sauce. Adjust the seasoning, cover the pan and simmer gently until the potatoes are cooked, about 10–15 minutes. This last stage of the cooking can be done in an earthenware casserole in the oven if preferred. Garnish with the parsley or basil and serve.

TARTE TATIN

CARAMELISED APPLE TART

Use apples that do not disintegrate easily when cooking.

185 g plain flour
125 g butter
2 teaspoons castor sugar
45 g ground almonds
1 egg yolk
1 tablespoon water
30 g extra butter
60 g extra castor sugar
1 kg apples

Serves 6–8

Preheat the oven to 200°C/400°F.

Sift the flour into a bowl and rub in the 125 g butter until crumbly. Add the 2 teaspoons of sugar and the almonds. Combine the egg yolk and the water and stir into the flour mixture. Knead lightly and leave to stand in a cool place.

Melt the 30 g butter in a 22-cm heatproof dish or cake tin. Add the 60 g sugar and allow to caramelise over a gentle heat taking care not to let it burn. Remove from the heat.

Peel, core and slice the apples. Pack them closely in the bottom of the dish, trying not to leave any gaps. Roll out the pastry to a circle slightly larger than the tin. Carefully cover the apples and tuck in around the edges of the dish.

Bake in the preheated oven for about 30–35 minutes. Allow to cool slightly and then turn out on to a serving dish, caramelised apple facing upwards. Serve warm or cold.

PETITS POTS AU CHOCOLAT À L'ORANGE

CHOCOLATE AND
ORANGE MOUSSE

125 g bitter, dark chocolate
rind of 1 large orange, finely grated
juice of 1 large orange
30 g unsalted butter
1 tablespoon brandy
3 eggs, separated

Serves 4

Break the chocolate into pieces and melt in a bowl over a pan of simmering water. Add the orange rind and juice together with the butter, mix well and then pour in the brandy.

Beat the egg yolks until smooth and fold in the chocolate mixture, stirring constantly until completely amalgamated. Allow the mixture to cool.

Whisk the egg whites until stiff and fold into the chocolate mixture. Pour into four small soufflé pots and chill before serving.

German cuisine is characterised by great diversity. This is perhaps not surprising, considering that modern Germany was formed from a large number of separate and often ancient states and that the central location of the country makes it a neighbour of almost all the nations of Western Europe.

Efficient German agriculture produces superb meats which are often smoked or pickled. German sausages (Wurst) are among the best in the world and even small towns and villages will have their own special varieties. The different types are far too numerous to mention individually but Bierwurst, Blutwurst, Weisswurst, Bratwurst, Knackwurst, Leberwurst, Mettwurst and Schinkenwurst are some of the better known. Wurst is often eaten with pickled vegetables, sauerkraut and cucumber.

Soups are popular too. They tend to be thicker in the north, being made from dried beans and lentils with the addition of sausages, potatoes and dumplings. Southern soups are lighter, often clear but also contain dumplings. Biersuppe is a speciality of Bavaria and combines lager, egg yolks, sugar, cream and cinnamon.

Goose is the traditional fare on Christmas day, stuffed with apples and onions and served with red cabbage. The neck may be stuffed with the minced liver, pork, truffles and herbs and is then fried in butter, to be eaten hot or cold. Even the legs are used, braised with onions and flavoured with vinegar and sugar. Hare and venison are also popular, cooked with wine and herbs.

Sauerkraut and potatoes are the most common vegetables, the latter being boiled, mashed and made into dumplings and potato cakes.

Sweets tend to be served in the afternoon with coffee, rather than as desserts at major meals.

Germany is famous for its beer and its annual beer festivals and German wines are among the finest in the world.

HEISSE BIERSUPPE

1 litre lager
100 g sugar
4 egg yolks, beaten
¼ cup sour cream
½ teaspoon ground cinnamon
salt and freshly ground black pepper

Serves 4

Heat the lager and the sugar in a large pan, stirring constantly until the sugar dissolves. Add the sour cream to the beaten egg yolks. Stir a couple of tablespoons of the hot beer into the egg and cream mixture. Whisk in the rest of the beer. Add the cinnamon and season with salt and pepper. Return to the heat and stir constantly until the soup thickens. Do not allow it to boil. Serve at once.

GULASCHSUPPE

This thick, hearty soup is better if made the day before it is required.

3 tablespoons oil
1 large onion, peeled and chopped
3 green peppers, seeded and chopped
3 tablespoons tomato paste
500 g lean beef, cut into bite-sized pieces
6 cups beef stock
1 teaspoon paprika
3 cloves garlic, peeled and crushed
1 tablespoon lemon juice
½ teaspoon caraway seeds
salt and freshly ground black pepper

Serves 4–6

Heat the oil in a large pan and cook the onion until transparent. Add the green peppers and stir in the tomato paste. Cover and simmer for 10 minutes. Add the chopped meat and stir until browned. Pour in the stock and add the remaining ingredients. Simmer for 1½ hours or until meat is tender. If desired, peeled and cubed potatoes can be added during the last 20 minutes of cooking time. Adjust seasoning before serving.

FRITTIERTE FRANKFURTER

150 g butter
1 onion, peeled and chopped
1 small green pepper, seeded and finely chopped
6 frankfurters, shredded
½ cup Parmesan cheese, grated
1 small bunch parsley, chopped
dash of Tabasco
6 eggs, beaten
salt and freshly ground black pepper

Serves 4

Melt the butter in a frying pan and sauté the onion and green pepper until soft. Add the shredded frankfurters and cook, stirring for about 5 minutes until browned.

Mix the Parmesan, parsley and Tabasco with the well beaten eggs and season with salt and pepper. Pour the eggs over the frankfurter mixture in the pan (it will resemble a large omelette). Cook until the eggs are set. Cut into wedges and serve with a salad.

ROTKOHL MIT BRATWURST

1 medium-sized red cabbage
2 large onions, peeled and chopped
2 large Granny Smith apples, cored and
    sliced but not peeled
3 tablespoons brown sugar
3 tablespoons cider vinegar
¾ cup chicken stock
1 dessertspoon caraway seeds
salt and freshly ground black pepper
1 kg bratwurst sausages
250 g bacon rashers

Serves 6

Preheat the oven to 150°C/300°F.

Cut the cabbage into quarters, remove the core and chop the leaves. Place the cabbage in a casserole with the onions, apples, sugar, vinegar, stock and caraway seeds. Season with salt and pepper and mix well. Cook for 3 hours, checking from time to time to ensure that all the moisture has not evaporated.

About 20 minutes before the cabbage is ready, cook the sausages and bacon rashers. Add to the cabbage mixture before serving.

SAUERBRATEN MIT KNÖDEL

MARINATED BEEF WITH DUMPLINGS

*This dish is left to sit in a marinade for
2–3 days, so allow time when planning its
preparation. It is traditionally served with
dumplings or noodles. (It is advisable not to use
an aluminium pan when cooking with vinegar.)*

1¾ cups red wine
¾ cup wine vinegar
2 onions, peeled and sliced
2 carrots, scraped and chopped
2 sticks celery, including tops, chopped
rind of ½ lemon
bouquet of herbs (2 bay leaves, 4 sprigs
    parsley, 2 sprigs thyme)
½ teaspoon allspice
4 cloves
1 teaspoon salt
½ teaspoon whole peppercorns
2 kg lean boneless beef
6 tablespoons butter
4 tablespoons plain flour
1 tablespoon brown sugar

Knödel   (Dumplings)
185 g plain flour
1½ teaspoons baking powder
½ teaspoon salt
freshly ground black pepper
pinch of mixed spice
45 g lard or butter
cold water

Serves 6

To prepare the marinade, combine the wine, vinegar, onions, carrots, celery, lemon rind, bouquet of herbs, allspice, cloves, salt and the peppercorns. Bring to the boil and simmer gently for 5 minutes.

Wipe the meat with a damp cloth, roll it up, fasten with string and place it in a large bowl. Pour the marinade over the meat and cover the bowl. Place it in the refrigerator and leave 2–3 days, turning from time to time. When you are ready to prepare the dish, remove the meat from the marinade and wipe dry.

Melt 4 tablespoons of the butter in a heavy pot and brown the meat on all sides. Remove the meat and sprinkle the pan with 2 tablespoons of the flour. Stir well. Pour the marinade into the pan, stirring constantly. Return the meat to the pan, cover and simmer gently for about 2½ hours, or until the meat is tender.

Melt the remaining butter in another pan and blend in the rest of the flour and the brown sugar. Stir over the heat until slightly browned. Skim any fat from the marinade, strain and gradually stir into the flour and sugar mixture and continue stirring until thick and smooth. Pour this sauce over the meat, cover and simmer for 30 minutes.

To make the dumplings, sift the dry ingredients into a bowl and mix the lard or butter in with the fingertips until the mixture resembles fine breadcrumbs. Add enough cold water to make the mixture into a firm, light dough. Divide the dough into 12 equal portions and roll into balls. Add to the top of the sauerbraten during the last ½ hour of simmering, cover and finish cooking.

FISCHFILLET IN DILLSOSSE

FISH FILLETS IN DILL SAUCE

Dill is a herb that is used often in recipes from northern Europe. Its special flavour has no substitute. Dried dill weed can be used if fresh dill is not available but you will only need half the quantity.

1 onion, peeled and sliced
bouquet of herbs (parsley, 1 bay leaf, thyme, piece of lemon rind)
1 wineglass white wine
2 cups water
salt and freshly ground black pepper
1½ kg white fish fillets

Sauce
¼ cup butter
1 small onion, peeled and finely chopped
2 tablespoons plain flour
2 tablespoons fresh dill, chopped
1 tablespoon parsley, chopped
½ cup sour cream
lemon juice
pinch of sugar
salt and freshly ground black pepper
2 egg yolks, beaten
parsley, chopped for garnishing

Serves 6

In a large shallow pan put the onion, bouquet of herbs, wine, water, salt and pepper and simmer for 10 minutes. Gently lower the fish into the pan and poach it until just cooked. Take the pan off the heat and keep warm.

To make the sauce, melt the butter and cook the onion gently for 5 minutes. Stir in the flour and cook for 2 minutes. Strain the liquid from the fish into the sauce, stirring constantly. Bring the mixture to the boil and cook rapidly to reduce it. When the sauce has thickened, add the herbs and cream and simmer for 5 minutes. Add the lemon juice and sugar, and adjust the seasoning. Add a little of the hot sauce to the beaten egg yolks and stir the egg mixture into the pan. Continue stirring until the sauce thickens, but do not boil or it will curdle. Pour the sauce over the fish and garnish with chopped parsley.

HASENPFEFFER

CASSEROLED HARE WITH BLACK PEPPERCORNS

You will need to start preparation of the hare 48 hours beforehand.

2 cups red wine
1 cup wine vinegar
8 black peppercorns
1 onion, peeled and stuck with 4 cloves
2 bay leaves
1 carrot, scraped and chopped
1 stick celery, chopped
1 large hare, jointed, or 2 rabbits, jointed (ask the butcher to do this)
2 tablespoons lard
6 rashers streaky bacon
1 tablespoon plain flour
1 tablespoon sugar

Serves 6–8

Make a marinade by putting the wine, vinegar, peppercorns, onion, bay leaves, carrot and celery into a pan. Bring to the boil and simmer gently for 15–20 minutes. Allow to cool. Place the hare or rabbit pieces in a large bowl and pour the marinade over them. Allow to stand for 48 hours, turning from time to time. Remove the meat from the marinade and dry on kitchen paper. Strain the marinade.

Preheat the oven to 180°C/350°F.

Melt the lard in a heavy pan and fry the meat, a few pieces at a time, until golden on all sides. Remove the rind from the bacon and place the rashers at the bottom of an earthenware casserole. Add the meat (reserve the pan with its juices) and season with salt and pepper. Sprinkle the flour and sugar into the pan in which the meat was browned and stir well with a wooden spoon. Return to the heat and slowly add the marinade, stirring all the time. When the liquid has thickened pour it over the meat pieces in the casserole. Cover and cook for about 2 hours, or until the meat is very tender.

KARTOFFELPUFFER

Served with bacon and a green salad, this dish makes a delicious, economical meal.

750 g potatoes, peeled
1 large onion, peeled
2 eggs, beaten
½ cup plain flour
salt and freshly ground black pepper
oil for frying

Serves 4

Coarsely grate potatoes and onions and mix together in a bowl. Add the beaten eggs and stir well. Fold in the flour and season with salt and pepper.

Heat a shallow layer of oil in a heavy based pan. When the oil is smoking add 2–3 tablespoons of the potato mixture and flatten with a spatula. When the underneath is crisp and brown, turn it over and cook on the other side.

Drain the potato cake on kitchen paper and keep warm while cooking the remainder of the mixture.

JERUSALEMER ARTISCHOCKENSALAT

500 g Jerusalem artichokes
4 anchovy fillets, chopped
salt and freshly ground black pepper

Mayonnaise
2 egg yolks
1 cup olive oil (approximately)
2 tablespoons wine vinegar
squeeze of lemon juice
salt and pepper

Serves 4

Wash the artichokes well under cold running water. (It is easier to peel them after they have been cooked.) Either cover with cold water and cook gently until tender, or steam until tender. Allow to cool, peel and slice. Season with salt and pepper and mix in the anchovies.

Mayonnaise is best made in a pestle and mortar, which should be warmed slightly under running water before use. Put the egg yolks in the bowl and stir until smooth. Add the olive oil, a drop at a time at first, building up to a trickle as the sauce amalgamates. When all the oil is added and the mayonnaise is thick and shiny, slowly add the vinegar and lemon juice and season with salt and pepper. Spoon over the artichokes and serve.

MARONEN MIT ÄPFELN

This sauce is served as an accompaniment to pork or ham.

500 g chestnuts
750 g apples, peeled, cored and sliced
sugar
salt

Make a slit at both ends of the chestnuts with a sharp knife and boil them in a large pan of water for 10–15 minutes. Allow the nuts to cool enough to handle and then remove the skins. Return to the pan, cover with fresh water and boil for about an hour until tender.

Cook the apples in a little water until soft and blend until smooth. Sweeten to taste with the sugar and add a pinch of salt. Add the chestnuts to the apple purée and mix.

ROSINENKUCHEN

250 g butter
6 eggs, separated
250 g castor sugar
½ teaspoon grated nutmeg
½ teaspoon ground cloves
pinch of salt
rind of ½ lemon, grated
375 g seeded raisins
250 g currants
1 cup rum
250 g self-raising flour, sifted

Serves 8–10

Preheat the oven to 150°C/300°F and grease a 22-cm cake tin.

Beat the butter until soft. Gradually add the egg yolks, sugar, nutmeg, cloves and salt. Beat until the mixture is smooth and creamy. Add the lemon rind, raisins, currants and three-quarters of the rum. Fold in the sifted flour. Whisk the egg whites until stiff and fold into the mixture.

Put the batter into the prepared cake tin, smooth the top, and make a depression in the centre. Bake for 2–2½ hours. While still warm sprinkle the top with the remaining rum. Leave for several days before cutting and the flavour of the cake will improve.

SCHWARZWÄLDER KIRSCHTORTE

This rich and quite delicious cake can be served with afternoon coffee, or as a splendid dessert.

Pastry Base
1 cup plain flour
¼ cup butter
3½ tablespoons sugar
1 tablespoon ground almonds
rind of ½ lemon, grated
1 egg yolk

Sponge
3 tablespoons plain flour
3 tablespoons cornflour
1 teaspoon baking powder
3 tablespoons cocoa
4 egg yolks
½ cup castor sugar
4 tablespoons hot water
4 egg whites
¼ cup butter, melted

Filling
500 g canned seeded cherries
2 tablespoons sugar
1 teaspoon lemon juice
2½ cups thick cream
3 tablespoons sugar
3 tablespoons kirsch
3 tablespoons dark chocolate, grated for decoration

Serves 8

Preheat the oven to 180°C/350°F and grease and lightly flour a round cake tin with a removable base.

To prepare the pastry base, sift the flour into a bowl and rub in the butter until the mixture is like fine breadcrumbs. Add the sugar, ground almonds and lemon rind and stir. Lastly add the egg yolk and mix to form a stiff dough. Roll into a ball, cover and refrigerate. When cool, roll the pastry to fit the base of the prepared tin. Bake in the preheated oven for about 20 minutes. Allow to cool slightly before removing it to a wire rack.

To prepare the sponge, clean the tin and grease and flour it again. Leave the oven at 180°C/350°F. Sift together the flour, cornflour, baking powder and cocoa. Beat the egg yolks and sugar with the hot water until thick and creamy. Whisk the egg whites until stiff. Fold the sifted flour, baking powder and cocoa into the egg yolk mixture with a metal spoon. Carefully fold in the egg whites, and lastly the melted butter. Bake in the prepared tin for about 35 minutes or until the cake has risen and springs back when pressed lightly in the centre. Allow to stand for a few minutes before transferring it to a wire rack to cool.

To make the filling, drain the cherries and place the syrup from the can with the sugar and lemon juice in a small pan. Simmer until thickened and add the cherries. In a separate bowl whip the cream until stiff and then add the sugar and kirsch.

To assemble the cake, place the pastry base on a large flat dish, spread with one-third of the whipped cream and spoon half the cherry mixture over it. Cut the chocolate cake in half and place one half on top of the cherries. Spread with half the remaining cream and add the rest of the cherry syrup. Top with the remaining layer of cake, decorate with the rest of the whipped cream and sprinkle with the grated chocolate. Chill before serving.

The culinary heritage of ancient Byzantium has influenced both Greek and Turkish food and it is sometimes difficult to differentiate between the two. Greek food today is characterised by its flavour, fragrance and the freshness of its ingredients.

The olive is a staple part of the Greek diet, being consumed both as a fruit and in the form of olive oil. Herbs grow wild in many areas and are widely used in the preparation of food. Vegetables such as tomatoes, aubergines, peppers and water melons, and fruits like peaches and grapes, add colourful touches to Greek meals.

A typical Greek salad comprises tomatoes, peppers, onions and olives, sprinkled with feta, a crumbly, salty cheese made from goat's milk.

Filo, a pastry as fine as tissue paper, is made into both savoury and sweet dishes. Perhaps the best known sweet is baklava, made from layers of filo brushed with melted butter and sprinkled with crushed walnuts, sugar and cinnamon. This is baked and while still warm, covered with a thick syrup made from sugar and water.

The Greeks love to eat outdoors and many tavernas allow the customers to personally select their meal from pots bubbling in the kitchen. Small bars abound, serving ouzo, an aperitif tasting strongly of aniseed, and retsina, a white wine made in resinated casks. Both tend to be an acquired taste.

PSAROSOUPA

1 kg of any firm white fish (including
    heads), scaled and cleaned
1 onion, peeled and chopped
1 leek, washed and chopped
2 cloves garlic, peeled and chopped
3 sticks celery, including tops, chopped
1 piece lemon rind
1¼ cups milk
2 tablespoons plain flour
¾ cup white wine
3 tablespoons tomato purée
salt and freshly ground black pepper
2 tablespoons chopped parsley
1 teaspoon chopped fennel

Serves 4–6

Put the fish, fish heads, onion, leek, garlic, celery and lemon rind into a large pan, cover with cold water and bring to the boil. Turn the heat down, cover and simmer until the fish is cooked. The time will depend on the type of fish: it is cooked when the flesh pulls away easily from the bone. Carefully remove the fish and allow it to cool. Continue to simmer the stock for about 20 minutes or until it has reduced by about one-third in volume. Meanwhile remove any skin and bones from the fish and break the flesh into large pieces. Strain the stock and return it to the pan.

Add the milk slowly to the flour and mix until it forms a smooth paste. Stir in the white wine and the tomato purée. Slowly add this mixture to the stock, stirring over a gentle heat until it thickens. Return the fish pieces to the soup and adjust the seasoning. Serve in bowls and sprinkle with the herbs.

SOUPA AVGOLEMONO

1.5 litres fish or chicken stock
90 g white rice
3 eggs
juice of 1 or 2 lemons

Fish Stock
1 kg fish pieces, including heads
2 litres water
½ cup wine vinegar
1 onion, peeled and stuck with 4 cloves
1 stick celery, including tops, chopped
1 carrot, scraped
6 peppercorns
bouquet garni

Serves 4–6

To make the stock, simmer all the ingredients in a large pot for about an hour. Strain and reduce to about 1.5 litres by simmering over a gentle heat. Adjust the seasoning.

To make the soup, bring the stock to the boil in a large pan. Add the rice and simmer until cooked—about 15 minutes. In a bowl whisk the eggs with the lemon juice, pour on a little of the hot soup and then add the mixture to the pot of hot soup. Do not allow the soup to boil, but continue to whisk until it thickens slightly.

KOLOKYTHIA KEFTETHES

3 potatoes
1 slice stale bread (3 cm thick)
2 cups zucchini or marrow, grated
2 onions, peeled and finely chopped
1 cup Parmesan cheese, grated
1 egg, beaten
1 teaspoon mint, finely chopped
1 dessertspoon parsley, chopped
salt and freshly ground black pepper
3 tablespoons flour
olive oil

Makes 12 rissoles

Peel, boil and mash the potatoes. Soak the bread in a little water and squeeze dry. Mix the zucchini, potatoes, onions and bread thoroughly. Add cheese, beaten egg, mint and parsley, season with salt and freshly ground pepper and mix well.

Take a spoonful of the mixture at a time and flatten into small patties. Dust the patties lightly with the flour and fry in hot olive oil until golden. Drain and serve while hot and crisp.

TARAMA KEFTETHES

Tarama is the salted and pressed roe of the grey mullet or cod. It is available in most good delicatessens.

1 large potato
2 slices white bread (3 cm thick)
1 medium onion, peeled
3 cloves garlic, peeled
250 g tarama
fresh mint
fresh parsley
pinch of cinnamon
pepper
plain flour
oil for frying

Serves 4

Peel, boil and mash the potato. Cut the crusts off the bread and discard. Soak the bread in water and squeeze dry. Put the onion, garlic, tarama, herbs, mashed potato and bread into a blender or fine mincer. Add a pinch of cinnamon and blend until thoroughly mixed. Season with pepper and leave to stand for 2 hours. Form the mixture into small flat cakes, coat in flour and fry in hot oil.

STIFATHO

1.5 kg stewing steak
oil for frying
400 g canned tomatoes
1½ wineglasses red wine
4 cloves garlic, peeled and crushed
bouquet of 2 bay leaves, 2 sprigs
    parsley, 2 sprigs thyme
1.5 kg pickling onions, peeled
½ wineglass wine vinegar
1 tablespoon sugar
1 small cinnamon stick
pinch of cummin
salt and pepper

Serves 4–6

Preheat the oven to 180°C/350°F.

Trim the meat of excess fat and cut into bite-sized pieces. In a large pan heat some oil and brown the meat lightly. Place in an earthenware casserole. Add the tomatoes, wine, garlic and the bouquet of herbs and cook in the oven for 1 hour. Add the onions, vinegar, sugar, cinnamon, cummin and season with salt and pepper. Return to the oven and cook for a further 2–2½ hours until the onions and meat are tender. Allow to stand for a short time before serving.

MOUSSAKA

Surely one of the delights of a Greek holiday must be the time spent strolling between the various tavernas sampling the exotic dishes. One of the most delicious of these is moussaka, made with that most splendid of vegetables—the aubergine—and cooked in a large copper pot.

2 kg aubergines
salt
oil for frying
1 large onion, peeled and chopped
1 kg minced beef
400 g canned tomatoes
2 tablespoons parsley, chopped

Preheat the oven to 220°C/425°F and grease a large baking dish.

Wipe and slice the aubergines, sprinkle them with salt and leave them to drain for ½ an hour to lose their bitterness. Rinse well and pat dry on kitchen paper. Heat some oil in a large frying pan and sauté the aubergines a few at a time until they are browned on both sides. Drain on kitchen paper and keep warm.

In another pan heat a little oil and sauté the onion until soft. Add the meat and brown. Stir in the tomatoes, parsley and cinnamon, season with salt and pepper and moisten with the wine. Cook slowly for 20 minutes. Remove from the stove and stir in a couple of tablespoons of the béchamel sauce.

Fill the greased baking dish with alternate layers of aubergines and the meat mixture, sprinkling each layer with a little grated cheese. The top and bottom layers should be of aubergines. Beat the eggs and fold into

½ teaspoon cinnamon
pepper
1 wineglass red wine
4 cups béchamel sauce (see page 69)
½ cup Parmesan cheese, grated
3 eggs
½ teaspoon nutmeg

Serves 6–8

the remaining béchamel sauce, add a little grated nutmeg and pour over the dish. Sprinkle the remaining cheese on the top and bake in a hot oven for about an hour. The top should be golden brown.

AVGOLEMONO SALTSA EGG AND LEMON SAUCE

This delicious sauce can be served with meat, fish or vegetables.

30 g butter
2 tablespoons plain flour
1¼ cups stock (fish or chicken)
2 eggs
juice of 2 lemons
2 tablespoons cold water

Serves 4

In a medium-sized pan melt the butter, stir in the flour and cook for a few minutes, stirring constantly. Remove the pan from the heat and add the stock, stirring all the time. Return to the heat and bring to the boil, stirring to prevent the sauce from becoming lumpy.

In a bowl, beat the eggs until frothy. Continue to beat while adding the lemon juice and cold water. Add several spoonfuls of the hot stock mixture to the egg and lemon mixture and blend. Now stir all the lemon mixture into the stock in the pan. Do not allow the sauce to boil or it will curdle.

TOMATES KE PIPERIES YEMISTES STUFFED TOMATOES AND PEPPERS

6 red or green peppers of uniform size
6 large tomatoes of uniform size
2 cups cooked rice
1 large onion, peeled and chopped
3 cloves garlic, peeled and crushed
2 tablespoons currants
1 cup cold lamb or chicken, minced
salt and freshly ground black pepper
olive oil

Serves 6

Preheat the oven to 180°C/350°F.

Cut the tops from the peppers and carefully remove the seeds and core. Blanch the peppers in boiling water for 5 minutes. Cut the tops from the tomatoes and scoop out the flesh.

Mix the tomato flesh with the rice, onion, garlic, currants and cold meat and season with salt and pepper. Stuff the tomatoes and peppers with this mixture and place them in an earthenware ovenproof dish. Pour a little olive oil over them and bake for about ½ an hour.

SPANAKORIZO SPINACH WITH ONIONS AND RICE

This dish can be served either hot or cold.

4 cups chicken stock
1 bunch spinach (about 375 g)
2 bunches spring onions
8 tablespoons olive oil
250 g long grain rice
salt and freshly ground black pepper
juice of 1 lemon

Serves 4–6

Heat the chicken stock and keep warm. Thoroughly wash the spinach and cook it in a large pan. There will be sufficient water clinging to the leaves after washing it to provide the moisture for cooking. Drain and cool. Squeeze out any excess moisture and chop.

Wash, trim and chop the spring onions—use both the green and white parts. Heat the oil in a heavy pan and cook the onions for 5 minutes. Add the spinach, stir and cook for another couple of minutes. Wash and drain the rice and add to the pan. Stir while continuing to cook for another 3 minutes.

Pour in the hot stock and simmer half covered until all the stock is absorbed (about 15 minutes.) By this time the rice should be cooked. Season with salt and pepper, and if serving cold squeeze the lemon juice over the top.

FASSOLIA YIACHNI

BEAN AND TOMATO STEW

In Greece, dishes such as this one are often served only lukewarm. This practice dates from earlier times when many families were without ovens and took their food to the local baker to be cooked.

1 kg runner beans
400 kg canned tomatoes
3 onions, peeled and chopped
1 cup olive oil
1 cup hot water
1 tablespoon sugar
2 cloves garlic, peeled and crushed
salt and pepper

Serves 4–6

Top and tail the beans and string if necessary. Cut each bean in half. Heat the oil in a large pan, add the onions and garlic and cook gently until soft. Add the beans, tomatoes, seasoning and hot water. Cover and simmer until tender. Remove from the heat and allow to stand for $\frac{1}{2}$ an hour before serving.

PRASSOPITTA

LEEK PIE

Filo is a Greek pastry which is as fine as tissue paper. It is used in many recipes—both savoury and sweet—and is readily available at most supermarkets and delicatessens.

2 kg leeks
3½ cups béchamel sauce (see page 69)
salt and pepper
nutmeg, grated
4 eggs
½ cup Parmesan cheese, grated
375 g filo pastry
90 g butter, melted

Serves 6–8

Preheat the oven to 180°C/350°C and grease a baking tin.

It is best if the leeks are prepared several hours before making the pie. Carefully wash the leeks, making sure you remove all the dirt. Discarding the green leaves, put the white parts in a large pan and cover with water. Cook until tender. Remove the leeks from the pan and when they are cool shred them with your fingers.

Make the béchamel sauce. In a separate bowl beat the eggs thoroughly and add them, with the grated cheese, to the béchamel sauce. Add the leeks and season with salt, pepper and grated nutmeg.

Line the baking tin with five or six sheets of the filo, painting each sheet with melted butter before adding the next. Spread the leek mixture evenly over the pastry and cover with the remaining filo, buttering each sheet as before. Fold in the edges to contain the filling, and score the top with a sharp knife. Brush the top sheet with melted butter and bake in the oven for about 1 hour, or until golden and crisp.

YAOURTI TZATZIKI

YOGHURT AND CUCUMBER SALAD

In Greece yogurt is used as a sauce, a dessert or a salad. It is also eaten for breakfast with the delicious, dark local honey.

1 large continental cucumber
2 cloves garlic
1 dozen fresh mint leaves
1 cup natural yoghurt

Serves 4

Finely slice the cucumber, peel and crush the garlic and finely chop the mint. Mix the ingredients together and serve as an accompaniment to grilled fish or kebabs.

YAOURTOPITA GLIKO

YOGHURT AND CITRUS DESSERT

2½ cups yoghurt
2 tablespoons castor sugar
rind of 1 lemon, grated
rind of 1 orange, grated
juice of 1 lemon or 1 orange
fresh mint leaves

Serves 4

Beat the yoghurt until smooth. Add the sugar, grated rind and juice and mix well. Chill and serve icy cold decorated with mint leaves.

BAKLAVA

LAYERED PASTRY WITH WALNUTS AND CINNAMON

250 g unsalted butter
1 cup castor sugar
1 cup hot water
2 cups chopped walnuts
500 g filo pastry
ground cinnamon

Syrup
1 cup castor sugar
1 cup honey
1 cup water
juice of 1 lemon

Serves 8–10

Preheat the oven to 180°C/350°F and grease a 25 × 30-cm baking tin.

To make the filling, heat half the butter with the sugar and hot water and add the chopped nuts.

Melt the remaining butter. Take a sheet of filo pastry, brush it liberally with melted butter and place it in a well buttered baking tin. Repeat with two or three more sheets, placing them one on top of the other. Spread a thin layer of the filling over the pastry, sprinkle with cinnamon and cover with three more sheets of buttered filo. Repeat this procedure, using alternate layers of filo and nuts. Make sure the final layer is at least four sheets thick. Tuck in the ends of the pastry, brush the top with melted butter and score into diamond shapes. Bake until golden.

To make the syrup, boil the sugar with the honey, water and lemon juice. Pour the syrup over the baklava while it is still hot.

HALVA

EASTER CAKE

125 g unsalted butter
250 g castor sugar
4 eggs, beaten
125 g ground almonds
250 g fine semolina
1 teaspoon cinnamon

Syrup
185 g sugar
1 cup water
juice of 1 lemon

Makes enough for 12 slices

Preheat the oven to 180°C/350°F and grease a 20-cm-square cake tin.

Beat the butter and sugar in a bowl until light and fluffy. Beat in the eggs then add the ground almonds, semolina and cinnamon and mix gently. Pour the mixture into the prepared tin and bake for 1 hour.

While the cake is cooking prepare the syrup. Bring the sugar, water and lemon juice to the boil and cook until the mixture begins to thicken. Allow to cool slightly before pouring over the cooked, warm halva. Slice and allow to cool before serving.

The climate of Holland can be harsh and Dutch meals are hearty. Warming soups and thick, rich stews are typical and whether one eats in a restaurant or in a private home, there is rarely any room left on the plate when the meal is served. Breakfasts are substantial, including eggs, cheese and a variety of cold meats, eaten with different kinds of bread, coffee or milk. Lunch can be a major meal comprising soup, seafood, red meat or ham, black bread and a little currant bread, finished off with cheese and fruit. For those with a more modest appetite, restaurants serve koffietafel or 'coffee table', a somewhat smaller offering. Dinner is the main meal of the day.

Holland's intimate association with the sea means that fish is always fresh and in abundant supply. Herring and eel are the most popular. Many vegetables thrive in the damp climate while others are grown in hothouses, making fresh produce available all year round. Plump white asparagus and cabbages are specialities.

The Dutch are famous for their rich dairy products. Among the best known are Edam, a round, firm cheese coated with red wax and a pale yellow cheese called Gouda. Both are exported throughout the world. Rich, creamy chocolates are also popular and are presented in many decorative ways.

In some areas, there is a distinct Indonesian influence, a reminder of the Dutch colonisation of the East Indies, and dishes such as nasi goreng are common.

Beer is drunk with most food. The locally produced gin (bols) comes in a variety of strengths and it is advisable to proceed with caution if sampling it for the first time.

HOLLAND: Ossetong met Rozynensaus (Ox-tongue with Raisin Sauce). See page 50.

SPINAZIE SOEP

Croutons
3 or 4 slices day-old bread
oil for frying

Soup
500 g spinach
30 g butter
1 tablespoon cornflour
½ cup milk
salt and freshly ground black pepper
nutmeg, grated
¾ cup cream

Serves 4

To make the croutons, remove the crusts from the bread and discard. Dice the bread or cut it into small triangles. Heat some oil in a small pan and cook the croutons, turning constantly, until brown. Drain on kitchen paper. These can be made in advance and stored in an airtight jar.

Wash the spinach thoroughly in cold water. Cook in a large saucepan with a little salted water and then purée in a blender. In another pan, melt the butter, mix in the cornflour and stir over the heat for about 1 minute. Gradually add the spinach purée, thinning with a little milk at the same time. Season with salt and pepper and a little grated nutmeg. Stir in the cream just before serving. Pour into bowls and add a few croutons.

BOERENKAASSOEP

4 rashers bacon, chopped
2 tablespoons butter
1 onion, peeled and chopped
2 tablespoons tomato paste
1 teaspoon hot mustard
1 teaspoon Worcestershire sauce
pinch of paprika
salt and freshly ground pepper
1 litre chicken stock
2 cups Edam cheese, grated
1 cup cream
1 cup milk

Serves 6–8

Sauté the bacon in a large pan until crisp, remove from the pan and drain. Melt the butter in the same pan and cook the onion until tender. Stir in the tomato paste, mustard, Worcestershire sauce and paprika and season with salt and pepper. Cook while stirring for 2 minutes. Slowly add the chicken stock, stirring until the soup boils. Cover and simmer for 30 minutes. Add the grated cheese and cook over a low heat until it has melted. Add the cream and milk, stirring to mix. Ladle into bowls and serve with croutons (see above).

ZUURKOOLSCHOTEL MET SPEK EN AARDAPPELEN

To the north of Amsterdam there is a region where cabbages grow in abundance. They are transported in small wooden boats along narrow canals to the factories where they are made into sauerkraut.

500 g sauerkraut
3 juniper berries, crushed
piece fat bacon (about 250 g)
¾ cup white wine
8 thin rashers bacon, rind removed
6 frankfurters
750 g small potatoes, peeled and boiled

Serves 4

Place the sauerkraut in the bottom of a heavy based pan. Add the juniper berries and place the piece of fat bacon in the centre. Pour on the wine and spread with the bacon rashers. Cover and cook over a gentle heat for 1 hour. Add the frankfurters and cook for another 20 minutes. Remove the fat bacon and slice. Arrange the sauerkraut on the bottom of a preheated serving dish. Place the sliced fat bacon on top and garnish with the frankfurters, bacon rashers and boiled potatoes.

GREECE: *Stifatho (Casserole of Beef with Onions and Wine). See page 44.*

OSSETONG MET ROZYNENSAUS   OX-TONGUE WITH RASIN SAUCE

1 ox-tongue
1 carrot, peeled and sliced
1 onion, peeled and stuck with 3 cloves
1 stick celery, including top, sliced
6 peppercorns, crushed
bouquet of herbs, including parsley,
    thyme and 1 bay leaf

Sauce
½ cup seedless raisins
½ cup port
3 tablespoons butter
3 tablespoons plain flour
2½ cups stock (reserved after cooking
    the ox-tongue)
1 tablespoon tomato purée
½ teaspoon sugar
1 teaspoon vinegar
salt and freshly ground black pepper

Serves 6–8

Soak the tongue for 3 hours in cold water and then rinse. Place the remaining ingredients in a large pot, add the tongue and cover with cold water. Put a lid on the pot and bring the liquid to the boil.

Reduce the heat and simmer gently until the thick end of the tongue is tender when pierced with a skewer (at least 2½ hours). Allow to cool slightly and then strain the liquid from the pan and reserve 2½ cups for the sauce. Remove the skin and any gristle from the tongue. Cut it into slices and keep warm.

To make the sauce, soak the raisins in the port for at least an hour and then strain, reserving both ingredients. In a small pan melt the butter, mix in the flour and stir over the heat for a minute or two. Gradually add the stock, stirring constantly until the sauce is smooth. Add the port, tomato purée, sugar and vinegar. Cook the sauce over a medium heat until it reduces a little in volume. Add the raisins and season with salt and pepper. Pour over the ox-tongue and serve with mashed potatoes.

APPELFLAPPEN   APPLE FRITTERS

2½ cups plain flour
pinch of salt
1¼ cups beer
6 cooking apples, peeled, cored and
    sliced
oil for frying
icing sugar

Makes about 30 fritters

Sift the flour and salt into a bowl, add the beer and beat until smooth. Allow this batter to stand for ½ an hour. Dip the apple slices into the batter and fry a few at a time in the hot oil until golden. Drain and dredge in icing sugar and serve while hot.

ONTBYTKOEK   HONEY CAKE

500 g liquid honey
1 cup nut or corn oil
4 eggs, well beaten
90 g light brown sugar
2 teaspoons ground cinnamon
½ teaspoon ground ginger
rind of 1 orange and 1 lemon, finely
    grated
2 teaspoons bicarbonate of soda
¾ cup cold strained tea
625 g plain flour

Serves 8–10

Preheat the oven to 180°C/350°F and grease and lightly flour a 22-cm cake tin.

Place the ingredients, with the exception of the flour, in a bowl, in the order in which they are listed. Beat until well mixed. Sift the flour and fold it into the mixture. You may need a little more or a little less flour—the batter should be rather moist. Bake in the oven for about 1¼ hours or until a skewer comes out clean when the cake is pierced. Allow to cool, wrap in foil and allow to stand for a few days before cutting. This will improve the flavour of the cake.

Hungarian food displays an artistry and delicacy that reflects the long cultural history of this sophisticated central European country. The Hungarian winter is severe, so it is no surprise that soups are thick and hearty or that goulash is a popular dish, often combining dumplings and noodles with sour cream and flavoured with paprika. The latter is fiery red and varies in strength from sweet and mild to very hot and is widely used in Hungarian cooking for both its colour and flavour. Another peculiarity of Hungarian cooking is the fact that lard is used in most dishes in preference to butter or oil.

Although Hungary has no sea coast, freshwater fish are plentiful and carp, perch, pike, sturgeon and trout are well known. Preserved vegetables are consumed in the winter months; sauerkraut is made in large quantities while red cabbage adds colour to many meals.

LIPTÓI KÖRÖZÖTT

CHEESE SPREAD

125 g unsalted butter (room
   temperature)
250 g cream cheese (room temperature)
250 g cottage cheese
2 tablespoons sour cream
1 tablespoon prepared mustard
2 tablespoons sweet paprika
freshly ground black pepper
1 tablespoon anchovy essence
1 tablespoon onion, grated
1 tablespoon capers
1 tablespoon caraway seeds

Makes 2½ cups

In a blender place the butter, cream cheese, cottage cheese and sour cream. Blend while adding the rest of the ingredients. Taste and adjust the seasoning if necessary. Pack the mixture into a container with a lid and refrigerate for 24 hours before use.

KÁPOSZTALEVES

SAUERKRAUT SOUP

2 tablespoons lard or oil
250 g boneless pork, finely chopped
1 onion, peeled and chopped
2 teaspoons sweet paprika
4 cups light stock
salt and pepper
1 can sauerkraut (about 400 g)
250 g smoked sausage, chopped
2 tablespoons plain flour
2 tablespoons water
sour cream

Serves 4

Heat the lard in a pan, add the pork and cook over a moderate heat until it has browned. Remove and drain on absorbent paper. Put the onion in the pan, cook until transparent and sprinkle in the paprika. Stir in the stock and the reserved pork and season with salt and pepper. Cover the pan and simmer gently for about an hour.

Drain the sauerkraut and rinse in a colander under cold running water. Add it to the soup with the chopped sausage and simmer for another 20 minutes. Mix the flour and water until you have a smooth paste, add to the soup and stir until it thickens. Serve in individual bowls topped with a dollop of sour cream.

TYUKHUSLEVES MÁJGALUSKÁVAL

CHICKEN BROTH WITH
LIVER DUMPLINGS

6 chicken livers, cleaned and rinsed
1 small onion, peeled
1 tablespoon butter, softened
1 egg, beaten
1 sprig fresh marjoram or ½ teaspoon
   dried marjoram
salt and freshly ground black pepper
1 tablespoon plain flour
½ cup dried breadcrumbs
1.5 litres chicken stock
2 tablespoons chopped parsley

Serves 4

Mince the chicken livers with the onion and add the butter, egg, marjoram and seasoning and mix well. Add the flour and enough breadcrumbs to form a stiff paste. Roll into small dumplings about the size of a walnut and refrigerate for an hour.

Bring the stock to the boil in a large pot. Drop the dumplings in a few at a time and cook for 10 minutes or until the dumplings rise to the surface. Remove with a slotted spoon and keep warm. Repeat this process until all the dumplings are cooked. Place them in a soup tureen and add the hot broth. Sprinkle with parsley and serve.

CITROMOS MARHASÜLT

LEMON BEEF

1 kg lean beef, cubed
1 cup beef stock
250 g bacon

Sauce
1 tablespoon butter or lard
1 tablespoon plain flour
stock reserved from beef
1 cup sour cream
1 teaspoon finely grated lemon rind
2 tablespoons lemon juice
1 teaspoon sugar
sprig chopped fresh tarragon or
    $\frac{1}{2}$ teaspoon dried tarragon

Serves 4

Put the meat and the stock in a heavy pot, cover and cook over a gentle heat until the meat is tender—about 45 minutes. Remove the meat and keep warm. In a separate pan, fry the bacon until crisp. Remove from the pan, drain, crumble and keep warm. Add the meat to the bacon fat in the pan and cook to brown it.

To prepare the sauce, melt the butter in a pan and add the flour. Stir constantly and cook until golden. Slowly add the stock, stirring all the time, until it boils and thickens. Lastly, add the sour cream, lemon rind and juice, sugar and tarragon. Heat but do not allow the sauce to boil. Place the meat on a warmed serving dish and spoon the sauce over it. Sprinkle with the crumbled bacon.

PAPRIKÁS CSIRKE

PAPRIKA CHICKEN

125 g butter or lard
2 onions, peeled and chopped
30 g paprika
4 tablespoons water
1 chicken (about 2 kg), cut into 8 pieces
3 green peppers
250 g tomatoes, peeled and chopped
salt and pepper
$\frac{3}{4}$ cup cream

Galuska   (Egg Dumplings)
500 g plain flour
2 eggs
water
60 g lard for frying

Serves 4

Melt the butter in a large pan and sauté the onions until soft. Add the paprika and mix well. Stir in the water and add the chicken pieces. Cover and cook gently for about 20 minutes. Remove the lid and raise the heat so that the liquid can evaporate a little.

Prepare the peppers by cutting them in half, removing the core and seeds and slicing into strips. Add the peppers and tomatoes to the chicken, season with salt and pepper, cover and cook for a further 15 minutes. Stir in two-thirds of the cream. Cover and keep warm.

To make the galuska, have ready a large pan of boiling salted water. Mix the flour and eggs together with a little water to form a soft dough. For the dumplings to be light they must be mixed quickly. Drop small pieces of the dough into the boiling salted water. Cook for three or four minutes and test to see if they are cooked through. Strain in a colander and rinse with cold water. Repeat until all the dumplings are cooked. Heat the lard until smoking and fry the dumplings for about 10 seconds. Keep hot until ready to serve.

Place the paprika chicken in a serving dish and spoon the remainder of the cream over the top. Serve the dumplings as an accompaniment.

GOMBAPAPRIKÁS

MUSHROOM PAPRIKA

Do not use the cultivated variety of mushroom for this dish as it does not have the same flavour.

500 g fresh field mushrooms
2 tablespoons butter or lard
1 small onion, peeled and chopped
1 teaspoon sweet Hungarian paprika
salt and freshly ground black pepper
1 tablespoon cornflour
1 cup sour cream

Serves 4

Wipe the mushrooms clean with a damp cloth and slice them. Melt the butter in a pan and sauté the onion until golden. Sprinkle with the paprika and cook, stirring for a few minutes. Add the sliced mushrooms, cover and sauté for about 5 minutes, or until the mushrooms are cooked. Season to taste with salt and pepper. Mix the cornflour with a little water until it forms a smooth paste, add to the mushrooms and stir until thickened. Lastly add the sour cream. Bring the mixture to the boil while stirring and remove from the heat at once.

TÖKFÖZELÉK

SWEET AND SOUR MARROW

2 kg marrow
salt
¼ cup butter or lard
1 large onion, peeled and chopped
1 tablespoon plain flour
125 g pickled dill cucumber
½ cup cucumber brine
⅔ cup sour cream
freshly chopped dill

Serves 6

Peel the marrow and shred it on a grater, taking care to discard the seeds. Place the grated marrow in a colander, sprinkle liberally with salt, cover with a plate and leave to drain for 1 hour. Place the colander under a tap of cold running water to remove the excess salt from the marrow and squeeze to remove as much liquid as possible.

Melt the butter in a pan and sauté the onion until it has softened. Mix in the flour and stir for 2 minutes over the heat. Place the cucumber and its brine in a blender and blend until smooth. Add the blended cucumber to the onion mixture, stirring constantly. When the mixture is smooth, spoon in the cream. Stir until simmering. Add the shredded marrow and bring to the boil, stirring until the marrow is just cooked. Do not let it get soggy. Adjust the seasoning and serve sprinkled with chopped dill.

TÖLTÖTT KÁPOSZTA

STUFFED CABBAGE ROLLS

1 large cabbage
500 g lean minced beef
1 onion, peeled and chopped
½ cup long grain rice
2 cloves garlic, peeled and crushed
½ cup sour cream
salt and pepper
1 can sauerkraut (about 400 g)
400 g canned tomatoes, sieved
1 bay leaf
sour cream for serving

Serves 4

Preheat the oven to 180°C/350°F.

Carefully remove about 16 leaves from the cabbage, discarding any damaged ones. Cut away the core from the centre of the leaves. Bring a large pan of water to the boil and simmer the leaves, a few at a time, for about 5 minutes. Remove and drain. Repeat until all the leaves are cooked.

In a large bowl combine the beef, onion, rice, garlic and sour cream. Season with salt and pepper and mix well. Take the drained cabbage leaves one at a time and spoon 2–3 tablespoons of the beef mixture on to each. Roll up like a small parcel and secure with a toothpick.

Place the sauerkraut in the bottom of an earthenware dish and sit the cabbage rolls on top, packing them neatly. Season the puréed tomato with salt and pepper and pour over the cabbage rolls. Put the bay leaf in the centre of the casserole. If the tomato does not cover the rolls completely, top up with a little water. Cover and cook in a moderate oven for 1–1½ hours. Remove from the oven, add more sour cream and serve.

SÓSKAFŐZELÉK

SORREL WITH SOUR CREAM

1 bunch sorrel (about 500 g)
1 tablespoon lard
1 small onion, peeled and finely
    chopped
¾ cup sour cream
1 tablespoon plain flour
salt
1 tablespoon sugar

Serves 4

Wash the sorrel in several changes of water. Melt the lard in a large pan and sauté the onion until soft. Add the sorrel, cover and cook over a gentle heat for 15 minutes. Place the sour cream in a bowl and fold in the flour. Add this to the sorrel and stir. Season with salt and sugar, purée in a blender and return to the stove. Simmer for 5 minutes and serve.

CSIPETKÉVEL

HARICOT BEANS WITH SOUR CREAM AND PAPRIKA

500 g haricot beans
1 bay leaf
2 sprigs fresh marjoram or ½ teaspoon
  dried marjoram
1 teaspoon salt
2–3 peppercorns
1 tablespoon lard
1 small onion, peeled and chopped
1 clove garlic, peeled and crushed
1 tablespoon plain flour
1 teaspoon paprika
¼ cup sour cream
½ teaspoon sugar
1 tablespoon vinegar

Serves 4

Soak the beans overnight in cold water. Drain them, cover with fresh water and add the bay leaf, marjoram, salt and peppercorns. Cover and simmer until tender. When cooked, drain the beans and remove the herbs and spices. Melt the lard in a pan and sauté the onion and garlic until soft. Sprinkle in the flour and paprika and cook, stirring for a couple of minutes. Put in the sour cream, sugar and vinegar and continue to cook, stirring the sauce until it begins to bubble. Add the beans, adjust the seasoning and stir to mix well.

KIFFELS

WALNUT PASTRIES

Pastry
250 g cream cheese (at room
  temperature)
⅔ cup butter (at room temperature)
2½ cups plain flour, sifted
icing sugar

Filling
1 egg white
250 g ground walnuts
½ cup castor sugar

Makes about 24 kiffels

Preheat the oven to 190°C/375°F and grease a baking tray.

Place the cream cheese, butter and flour in a bowl and work together with your hands until the mixture forms a stiff dough. Roll into a ball, cover and refrigerate overnight.

To prepare the filling, beat the egg white until stiff, add the walnuts and sugar and mix well.

Dust the surface of a board with icing sugar and roll out the pastry. With a pastry cutter or large glass cut out circles. Place a teaspoon of the filling in the centre of each circle, fold the pastry over and secure the edges by pinching them (they should look like semicircles). Place the kiffels on the greased tray and bake for about 20–25 minutes or until lightly browned.

MANDULÁS

ALMOND PUDDING

1 heaped tablespoon ground almonds
90 g butter (at room temperature)
90 g castor sugar
90 g plain flour
1½ cups milk
90 g slivered almonds
4 egg yolks
4 egg whites

Serves 4

Preheat the oven to 180°C/350°F.

Butter four small soufflé dishes (or one large 18-cm dish) and dust lightly with the ground almonds. Cream the butter with 60 g of the sugar, and fold in the flour along with the milk and the slivered almonds. Place the mixture in a saucepan and cook over a low heat, stirring until it thickens. Remove from the heat and add the egg yolks, one at a time, stirring after each additon. Whisk the whites in a bowl until stiff, fold in the remaining sugar and stir into the almond mixture. Make sure the ingredients are amalgamated before spooning into the soufflé dishes. Stand the dishes in a pan of cold water and bake in a moderate oven for 35–40 minutes.

If preferred this pudding can be steamed in a double boiler. The cooking time will be the same. Fresh cream, whisked with a little vanilla, can be served as an accompaniment.

The most outstanding feature of Indian cooking is the use of spices. As whole spices keep their flavour far longer than the ground product, they are usually stored whole and ground by the cook only when required.

Indian food varies greatly according to region. Generally, the food of northern India is richer than that of other areas; it includes more meat and wheat rather than rice and consequently bread is an important part of the diet.

Much of the Indian population is vegetarian, for economic as well as religious reasons. There tend to be more vegetarians in the south where the staple diet is rice and other grains, lentils and vegetables. Food becomes hotter the further south you travel.

Where meat is eaten, it is most commonly goat, sheep or chicken; all tend to be rather tough so long, slow cooking is required. In areas where bread is a staple, it is home made without yeast and fried rather than baked. The flat, round chapati is the best-known type. Widely-grown fruits include oranges, mangoes and papaws.

The way in which meals are served also varies in different parts of the country. In the north, all the dishes are placed on the table at the same time. In central India everyone is provided with a round tray containing a number of small dishes and at least one kind of spicy relish. In the south a banana leaf serves instead of a plate, with a 'well' in the centre containing various additions to the meal. Food is eaten with the right hand only.

GARAM MASALA GROUND MIXED SPICES

1 tablespoon black peppercorns
1 tablespoon coriander seeds
3 teaspoons caraway seeds
2 teaspoons cardamom seeds
1 teaspoon cloves
piece cinnamon stick 2 cm long

This is a mixture of ground spices. They can be bought already ground and packaged, or if you wish you can prepare the mixture yourself. Grind the spices in a mortar with a pestle until they are mixed well. If not used all at once store in an airtight jar.

SAMOSAS CURRY PUFFS

2 tablespoons ghee or butter
8 spring onions, chopped
2 cloves garlic, peeled and crushed
1 teaspoon fresh ginger, finely chopped
1 teaspoon curry powder
pinch of cinnamon
250 g lamb, minced
salt and freshly ground black pepper
juice of $\frac{1}{2}$ lemon

Pastry
500 g plain flour
$\frac{3}{4}$ cup natural yoghurt

Serves 6

Heat the ghee and sauté the spring onions with the garlic and ginger until soft. Add the curry powder and cinnamon and cook, stirring for 5 minutes. Put in the meat and continue stirring until it is cooked. Season with the salt and pepper and squeeze lemon juice over the top.

To prepare the pastry, sift the flour into a bowl and add enough of the yoghurt to make a pliable dough. It should not be sticky. Lightly dust a board with flour and roll out the pastry. Cut out circles with a small glass or pastry cutter. Place a spoonful of the filling in the centre of each, fold over the pastry to enclose the filling and pinch together to seal.

Heat a pan of oil until smoking and deep fry the curry puffs, a few at a time, until golden. Drain and serve with a chutney or relish.

KOFTA KARI CURRIED MEAT BALLS

$\frac{1}{2}$ onion, peeled and grated
$\frac{3}{4}$ teaspoon ground coriander
1 teaspoon dry mustard
$\frac{1}{2}$ teaspoon ground cummin
$\frac{1}{2}$ teaspoon ground ginger
$\frac{1}{2}$ teaspoon chilli powder
1 clove garlic, peeled and crushed
500 g lean beef, finely minced
1 dessertspoon yoghurt
1 egg, beaten

Curry Sauce
5 tablespoons ghee
1 large onion, peeled and sliced
$\frac{1}{2}$ teaspoon cayenne pepper
$\frac{1}{2}$ teaspoon cummin
$\frac{1}{2}$ teaspoon turmeric
$\frac{1}{2}$ teaspoon ground coriander
1 teaspoon ground ginger
400 g canned tomatoes
3 cloves garlic, peeled and crushed
3 cups cold water

Serves 4

Melt a little ghee in a pan and fry the onion, spices and garlic. Stir and cook for about 5 minutes over a gentle heat to blend the spices. Remove from the heat and allow to cool. Add the meat, yoghurt and egg and season with salt. Mix thoroughly. Shape the mixture into small balls. In a clean pan heat some more ghee and fry the koftas, turning them so that they brown evenly. Drain on absorbent paper.

To prepare the curry sauce, melt the ghee and sauté the onion until soft. Add the spices, tomatoes and garlic. Cook for about 10 minutes. Add the water and bring to the boil. Gently drop the koftas into the sauce and simmer for another 15 minutes. Lower the heat, cover the pan and cook for another 10 minutes. The ghee will float on the top of the dish. When serving, break through this film and serve the koftas and sauce from underneath.

SHAMMI KABAB

LAMB PATTIES

1 green chilli
2 onions, peeled and chopped
2 cloves garlic, peeled and crushed
1 kg minced lamb
2 tablespoons ground coriander
2 tablespoons chopped parsley
2 teaspoons ground ginger
1 teaspoon turmeric
salt
3 tablespoons plain flour
oil or ghee for frying

Serves 6–8 (makes 16 patties)

Remove the seeds from the chilli and chop the flesh finely. Place in a bowl with the chopped onion, garlic and the minced lamb. Add the coriander, parsley, ginger and turmeric and season with salt. Add the flour, stirring until well distributed. Form the mixture into about 16 balls and flatten each one slightly. Heat the oil in a frying pan and cook the patties for about 5 minutes on each side. Serve hot with natural yoghurt.

TANDOORI MURGH

TANDOORI CHICKEN

1 large chicken, cut into serving pieces
1 small piece fresh ginger, peeled
1 small onion, peeled and chopped
3 cloves garlic, peeled
1 teaspoon coriander
$\frac{3}{4}$ cup natural yoghurt
$\frac{1}{2}$ teaspoon salt
1 teaspoon chilli powder
$\frac{1}{2}$ teaspoon black pepper
pinch of red colouring (available at
    stores selling Asian foods)

Serves 4

For complete authenticity this dish should be cooked in a special oven lined with mud and cow dung. However, it still has a good flavour when cooked over charcoal, or grilled.

Place all the ingredients (except the chicken) in a blender and blend until you have a smooth paste. Remove the skin from the chicken and slash the flesh with a sharp knife. Marinate the chicken pieces in the yoghurt and spice mixture for a minimum of 6 hours and up to 24 hours if possible. Shake the excess marinade from the chicken and grill under a fierce heat, lowering the temperature after the first 5 minutes. Turn the chicken pieces over when they start to blacken. Cook for about 35 minutes, or until the juices run clear when pierced with a skewer. Serve with rice and mint chutney.

CHANNA DAHL

SAVOURY CHICK PEAS

150 g chick peas
$\frac{1}{4}$ teaspoon bicarbonate of soda
3 tablespoons ghee or cooking oil
$\frac{1}{4}$ teaspoon cummin seeds
2 cloves garlic, peeled and crushed
1 slice fresh root ginger about 2 cm
    thick, finely chopped
1 onion, peeled and chopped
2 teaspoons garam masala (see page 57)
1 teaspoon ground coriander
1 tablespoon tomato purée
1 teaspoon salt
$\frac{1}{4}$ teaspoon cayenne pepper
1 tablespoon lemon juice

Serves 4

Soak the chick peas with the bicarbonate of soda in cold water overnight. Put the chick peas and their water in a pan, bring to the boil and remove any scum. Simmer with the lid on for about an hour, or until tender. Check occasionally to see that the peas remain covered with water.

Heat the ghee in a pan and fry the cummin seeds until they start to darken. Add the garlic, ginger and onion and fry until the onion begins to brown. Reduce the heat and add the garam masala, coriander, tomato purée, salt, cayenne pepper and lemon juice. Stir well. Finally add the cooked chick peas and about $\frac{1}{4}$ cup of their cooking liquid. Cover and simmer for about $\frac{1}{2}$ an hour, stirring from time to time.

GOBI KARI CAULIFLOWER CURRY

1 large cauliflower
2 tablespoons ghee or butter or
    vegetable oil
1 onion, peeled and chopped
1 dessertspoon garam masala (see
    page 57)
1 teaspoon ground mustard seed
½ teaspoon ground chilli
½ teaspoon ground turmeric
salt
¾ cup water

Serves 4

Remove the stalk from the cauliflower and cut the flowers into pieces. Melt the ghee and cook the onion gently for 5–10 minutes. Add the ground spices and the cauliflower pieces and stir for 3–4 minutes. Season with salt and add the water. Cover and cook until the water has evaporated, stirring from time to time.

USAL GREEN BEANS WITH MUSTARD

¼ fresh green chilli
500 g green beans
2 tablespoons yoghurt
½ tablespoon dry English mustard
1 tablespoon green coriander leaves,
    finely chopped
½ teaspoon ground cummin
¼ teaspoon sugar
2 teaspoons lemon juice
2 tablespoons water
salt
3 tablespoons ghee or cooking oil
½ teaspoon fenugreek seeds

Serves 4

Remove the seeds from the chilli and chop the flesh finely. Top and tail the beans, and string if necessary. In a bowl mix together the yoghurt, mustard, coriander leaves, cummin, sugar, lemon juice and water. Season with salt. Heat the ghee or oil in a pan and fry the fenugreek seeds and chilli until they begin to brown. Add the beans and stir. Spoon in the yoghurt mixture, bring to the boil, cover and simmer for about 30 minutes, stirring from time to time. By the end of the cooking time all the liquid should have evaporated.

NARIYAL KA DOODH COCONUT MILK

Coconut milk is not, as some may imagine, the watery liquid inside the coconut. It is a milk made from the coconut flesh. It must be stirred continuously when cooking or it will curdle. If possible use freshly grated coconut flesh, although desiccated coconut can be substituted.

**freshly grated flesh of 1 coconut or 2
    cups desiccated coconut
1 cup warm water**

Place the coconut in a bowl and add half the water. Using your fingers squeeze the coconut and water together. Allow to stand for 20 minutes and squeeze once more. Strain the resulting liquid into a container. Add the remainder of the water and repeat the process. Finally, press the coconut in a sieve to extract any remaining moisture.

PODINA CHATNI

¾ cup natural yoghurt
1 bunch mint
pinch ground cummin
salt

Place the yoghurt in a bowl. Finely chop the mint leaves—you will need about a handful—and put in the bowl. Add the cummin and season with salt. Serve in a small dish to accompany curries and other dishes.

KHIRA RAITA

½ cucumber
1 cup natural yoghurt
1 clove garlic, peeled and crushed
¼ teaspoon ground cummin
¼ teaspoon caraway seeds
salt and freshly ground pepper
pinch of paprika

Serves 4

Grate the cucumber. Put the yoghurt in a bowl and mix in the cucumber and all the remaining ingredients (except the paprika). Season with salt and freshly ground pepper. Sprinkle with the paprika just before serving.

KELA HALWA

25 g butter
75 g semolina
2 ripe bananas, peeled and mashed
4 cardamom seeds, crushed
50 g brown sugar
3 tablespoons water
100 g creamed coconut
1 tablespoon flaked almonds

Makes about 16 pieces

Grease a shallow 15 × 22-cm tin.

Melt the butter in a small pan and add the semolina. Cook over a gentle heat, stirring constantly, until the semolina turns golden. Mix in the mashed bananas.

Cook the sugar and water in a small pan over a gentle heat, stirring until the sugar has dissolved. Add the coconut and stir until it has mixed into the liquid. Now add the semolina and banana mixture, continue cooking and stir constantly. As soon as the mixture thickens and comes away from the sides of the pan, spoon it into the prepared tin. Spread the fudge evenly, sprinkle with the cardamoms and flaked almonds and press them into the surface. When the fudge is cool cut it into squares and store in a cool place.

GAJJAR KHEER

500 g carrots, grated
1¼ cups milk
125 g sugar
pinch of ground cardamom
60 g butter
cream for serving

Serves 4–6

Put the carrot into a pan with the milk and sugar and simmer, uncovered, until the milk has been absorbed—about 1 hour. Stir occasionally during this time. When the milk has been absorbed add the cardamom and the butter and cook until this has been amalgamated, and the carrots are beginning to look darker and transparent. Serve hot with cream.

The Republic of Indonesia comprises more than 13 000 islands, scattered over a length of some 4000 kilometres. Once known to Europeans as the 'Spice Islands', Indonesia was the principal source of Europe's exotic spices for over 300 years. While the food of each area varies according to what is available locally, spices including chilli, ginger, coriander, cinnamon and turmeric are used extensively throughout Indonesia along with coconut milk, lemons and limes.

Indonesians have a great sense of colour and design and this is reflected in the importance they place on the preparation and presentation of their food. Meat is expensive and eaten only in small quantities, usually finely sliced or added to a dish consisting mainly of rice or noodles. Saté, small cubes of meat threaded onto bamboo skewers and then barbecued and served with peanut sauce, is considered the national dish. Poultry and eggs are also important items of diet. Many Indonesians are Moslems and therefore do not eat pork. However, the inhabitants of Bali are Hindus and do use pork prepared in a number of ways, including spit-roasted sucking-pig that is cooked on special occasions.

Every meal is served with at least one sambal, a hot or spicy relish or sauce, presented in a small bowl. Some Indonesian dishes are pungently hot and it is advisable to adjust the amount of chilli used to suit the individual palate. Desserts are rare and a meal is normally finished off with fresh fruit. Depending on the season, this might include papaya (papaw), banana, mango, pineapple, watermelon, salak (a small, brown pear-shaped fruit with skin like a crocodile and firm flesh surrounding a large brown seed) or durian, a fruit loved by many but possessing a smell that can shock and surprise!

SOTO AYAM

1 large chicken (about 1.5 kg)
1 onion, peeled and chopped
2 sticks celery, including tops, chopped
1 teaspoon black peppercorns
1 teaspoon salt
2 tablespoons oil
1 extra onion, peeled and chopped
1 teaspoon finely chopped ginger
1 clove garlic, peeled and crushed
1 red chilli, seeded and finely chopped
½ teaspoon ground turmeric
1 tablespoon ground coriander
1 teaspoon ground cummin
½ teaspoon ground mace
salt and freshly ground pepper

Suggested Garnishes
3 eggs, hardboiled, peeled and chopped
1 small bunch spring onions, chopped
110 g noodles, cooked
60 g bean sprouts
sambals (see pages 64 and 65)
wedges of lime or lemon

Serves 6

Place the chicken in a large pan with one chopped onion, celery, peppercorns and salt. Cover with cold water, bring to the boil, reduce heat and simmer until tender—about 1 hour. Allow to cool slightly. Remove the chicken and reserve the stock. Cut the chicken meat into pieces, removing the skin and bones.

Heat the oil in a large pan and sauté the onion, ginger, garlic and chilli. When the onion is soft add the turmeric, coriander, cummin and mace and continue to cook, stirring, for 2 minutes. Add the strained chicken stock and the chicken meat. Adjust the seasoning and simmer for 20 minutes. Prepare the individual garnishes, place in separate bowls and serve with the soup.

This is really a complete meal in itself. Traditionally, the bowl of soup is put in the centre of the table and the garnishes are placed in surrounding dishes. The desired garnish is spooned into the bottom of a bowl and the hot soup is poured on top.

BAWANG GORENG

oil for frying
2 onions, peeled and sliced evenly

Heat the oil in a heavy based pan and fry the onions. Stir them constantly, turning them so that they brown evenly. Drain and store in an airtight jar. They should be brown and crisp. Use as a garnish.

REMPEYEK UDANG

175 g plain flour
50 g rice flour
½ teaspoon salt
½ teaspoon chilli powder
½ teaspoon ground cummin
½ teaspoon ground coriander
1 egg, beaten
½ cup water
½ teaspoon prawn paste
1 small onion, grated
1 clove garlic, peeled and crushed
500 g prawns, peeled, de-veined and
    finely chopped
oil for frying

Serves 4

Sift the flour, rice flour, salt, chilli powder, cummin and coriander together. Make a well in the centre and add the egg, water and prawn paste and mix until smooth. Allow to stand for 20 minutes and then add the onion, garlic and prawns. Mix well. If the batter is too stiff add a little more water. Heat about ½ cup of oil in a medium-sized pan (the oil should be about ½ cm deep). Drop the batter into the hot oil, about 2 tablespoons at a time. Turn the fritters to brown on both sides, remove from the pan and drain on absorbent paper. Repeat until all the fritters are cooked.

DADAR

OMELETTE

2 tablespoons grated onions
2 fresh chillies, finely chopped
8 eggs, beaten
2 tablespoons water
salt and pepper
oil or butter

Serves 4

Place the onion and chilli in a bowl with the eggs and mix. Add the water and season with salt and pepper. In a large, heavy based omelette pan heat about a tablespoon of oil (enough to make a thin film over the bottom of the pan). Add half the egg mixture and cook until the omelette is set and the base is browned. Fold and serve at once. Repeat the process with the remaining half of the mixture. Each omelette will serve two people.

IKAN BUMBU SANTAN

FISH IN HOT COCONUT SAUCE

750 g bream fillets (or other fish of your choice)
salt and freshly ground black pepper
4 tablespoons plain flour
oil for frying

Sauce
oil for frying
2 onions, peeled and chopped
1 clove garlic, peeled and crushed
1 red chilli, seeded and finely chopped
1 teaspoon chilli powder
1 small piece fresh ginger (about 3 cm), finely chopped
½ teaspoon shrimp paste
3 tomatoes, peeled, seeded and chopped
1 green pepper, seeded and chopped
1 bay leaf
pinch of ground turmeric
1½ cups coconut milk (see page 59)

Serves 4

Make the sauce first. Heat a little oil and sauté the onion, garlic and chopped chilli until golden. Add the chilli powder, ginger, shrimp paste, tomatoes and pepper and cook over a gentle heat for 5 minutes. Add the bay leaf, turmeric and coconut milk, stir until almost boiling, reduce the heat and simmer until the sauce is thick. Keep warm while preparing the fish.

Rinse the fish and cut it into pieces about 8 cm long. Add a little salt and pepper to the flour and lightly dust the fish pieces. Heat enough oil in a large pan to fry the fish. When golden drain it on kitchen paper. Arrange the fish on a serving dish and pour the hot sauce over the top.

SATÉ KAMBING

LAMB OR MUTTON SATAY

1 kg boneless lamb or mutton, cut into small cubes

Marinade
1 onion, peeled and finely chopped
2 cloves garlic, peeled and crushed
1 teaspoon coriander seeds, crushed
pinch of cayenne pepper
1 tablespoon honey
3 tablespoons lemon juice
2 tablespoons brown sugar
2 tablespoons soy sauce
salt and freshly ground black pepper

Serves 6

Saté is one of the more popular Indonesian dishes. Meat is threaded onto bamboo skewers and grilled over hot coals and dipped into a sauce. The sauces usually have a peanut base and range from mild to fiery in strength.

Combine all the ingredients to make the marinade. Mix well and marinate the cubed meat for at least 2 hours. Thread the meat on wooden skewers and grill until cooked.

LAPIS DAGING SEMARANG

SEMARANG-STYLE SLICED BEEF

The meat used in Indonesian food is mainly mutton, lamb, beef, buffalo and goat. It tends to be tough and is fairly expensive. Usually it is served in small quantities, finely sliced.

1 onion, peeled and finely chopped
2 cloves garlic, peeled and crushed
3 tablespoons soy sauce
1 teaspoon cinnamon
$\frac{1}{4}$ teaspoon freshly grated nutmeg
freshly ground black pepper
500 g beef, sliced thinly and cut into
   5-cm lengths
2 tablespoons oil
1 onion, peeled and sliced
2 tomatoes, peeled and chopped

Serves 4

In a large bowl make a marinade with the chopped onion, garlic, soy sauce, cinnamon and nutmeg. Season with pepper, add the sliced beef and stir to coat all the pieces. Allow to stand for about 2 hours. Heat the oil in a large pan and sauté the sliced onion until golden. Add the meat and the marinade and cook for 5 minutes, stirring constantly. Add the tomatoes, reduce the heat, cover and cook until the meat is tender— about 40 minutes.

ROTI JALA

LACE PANCAKES

These pancakes are given their lacy appearance by allowing the batter to drop from the fingers of one hand into the frying pan. The procedure is less messy if a perforated ladle is used.

250 g plain flour
pinch of salt
2 eggs, beaten
1$\frac{1}{2}$ cups milk or water or coconut milk
   (see page 59)
oil for frying

Serves 4–6

Sift the flour and salt into a bowl and make a well in the centre. Add the eggs and milk and mix to make a smooth batter. Lightly grease a pan with a heavy base. Heat the pan and drop the batter into it through a perforated ladle. Turn and cook on the other side. Remove from the pan and drain. Continue until all the batter is used. Serve with curries.

SAMBAL GORENG UDANG

PRAWN AND CHILLI SAUCE

This sauce can be covered and stored in the refrigerator.

125 g dried prawns
hot water
3 tablespoons oil
1 onion, peeled and grated
3 tablespoons finely chopped fresh
   chilli
2 teaspoons salt
1 tablespoon coconut milk (see
   page 59)
lemon or lime juice, freshly squeezed

Put the prawns in a bowl, pour hot water over them and soak until soft. Mince. Heat the oil in a small pan and sauté the onion and chilli until soft. Add the salt and the prawns and cook, stirring until well mixed. Add the coconut milk and cook, stirring until the sauce becomes dry. Squeeze with lemon juice and serve.

GERMANY: Schwarzwälder Kirschtorte (Black Forest Cake). See page 41.

SAMBAL TOMAT

½ dried chilli
2 tomatoes, peeled and chopped
½ teaspoon ground ginger
1 tablespoon water
1 teaspoon shrimp paste
½ teaspoon salt

Soak the chilli in water for 10 minutes and then place all the ingredients in a blender and blend until smooth.

NASI GORENG

3 tablespoons oil
1 onion, peeled and chopped
2 cloves garlic, peeled and crushed
1 teaspoon chilli, finely chopped
½ teaspoon shrimp paste
6 cups cooked rice
salt
1½ tablespoons soy sauce
prawns, beef, pork or chicken
   (optional)
peanuts or fried onion flakes (see page
   62) for garnishing

Serves 4

Heat the oil in a medium-sized pan. Sauté the onion, garlic and chilli until soft and then stir in the shrimp paste. Add the rice, season with salt and heat, stirring until all the rice is coated with the oil mixture. Add the soy sauce and mix well. (If desired, small shelled prawns or finely sliced beef, pork or chicken can be added at the same time as the soy.) Garnish with peanuts or fried onion flakes.

BAKMIE GORENG

This traditional Indonesian dish is versatile in that you can use the meat and vegetables of your choice.

250 g thin egg noodles
1 egg, beaten
2 tablespoons vegetable oil
1 onion, peeled and chopped
2 cloves garlic, peeled and crushed
125 g raw chicken, chopped
125 g raw prawns, shelled and de-
   veined
½ red chilli, seeded and finely chopped
1 stick celery, chopped
4 spring onions, chopped
90 g Chinese cabbage, chopped
2 tablespoons soy sauce
1 teaspoon salt
1 teaspoon sugar
fried onion flakes (see page 62)

Serves 4

Cook the noodles in plenty of boiling salted water. Do not overcook. Drain and reserve. Make the beaten egg into a thin omelette. When cool, shred and reserve.

In a large pan heat the oil and sauté the onion, garlic, chicken and prawns until cooked. Add the chilli, celery, spring onions and cabbage and fry, stirring for a few minutes. Quickly add the noodles, soy sauce, salt and sugar and stir. Cook only until the dish is heated through. It is important that the vegetables retain their crispness and colour, so a minimum amount of cooking is required. Garnish with the shredded omelette and onion flakes.

ITALY: *Aranci Caramellizzati (Caramelised Oranges). See page 71.*

SAUS BUMBU KACANG

MILD PEANUT SAUCE

1–2 tablespoons peanut oil
1 onion, peeled and chopped
pinch of chilli powder
250 g peanuts fried in 1 tablespoon oil
    or 250 g crunchy peanut butter
1 cup water
1 teaspoon brown sugar
juice of $\frac{1}{2}$ lime or $\frac{1}{2}$ lemon
1 tablespoon soy sauce
salt

Heat the oil in a pan and sauté the onion until golden. Add the chilli powder, peanuts, water and sugar. Bring to the boil while stirring and continue to cook until the mixture is thick and smooth. Add the lime juice and soy sauce. Taste and add salt if necessary. Serve with saté.

REMPEYEK KACANG

PEANUT CRISPS

1 cup rice flour
1 tablespoon cornflour
$\frac{1}{2}$ cup warm water
2 teaspoons coriander
2 cloves garlic, peeled
$\frac{1}{2}$ small onion, peeled and grated
1 cup boiling water
1 cup raw peanuts
1 teaspoon salt
lard or oil for frying

Makes 18 crisps

Mix the rice flour, cornflour and warm water until you have a smooth thick paste. In a separate bowl grind the coriander, garlic and onion and add to the paste. Add the cup of boiling water, stirring constantly to avoid lumps. Lastly stir in the peanuts and salt. Deep fry spoonfuls in a pan of hot lard or oil. When crisp remove the crisps with a slotted spoon and drain.

LEPAT NAGASARI

COCONUT CUSTARD WITH BANANAS

In Indonesia this dessert would normally be served in small cups made of banana leaves. Small bowls can be substituted.

2 large ripe bananas
75 g creamed coconut
2 cups water
125 g castor sugar
pinch of salt
$\frac{1}{2}$ teaspoon vanilla essence
250 g rice flour

Serves 6

Place the unpeeled bananas in a large pan and cover with cold water. Bring to the boil and simmer for 5 minutes. Remove from the heat and allow to cool.

Dissolve the creamed coconut in the 2 cups of water over a gentle heat, add the sugar, salt and vanilla and cook for a further 5 minutes. Allow to cool slightly. Carefully add the rice flour, taking care it does not become lumpy. Return to the heat and cook until the mixture becomes transparent. Divide the mixture between 6 small bowls and serve garnished with the bananas, peeled and sliced. Serve cold.

Italians enjoy food with the same gusto that they enjoy life. Italian cooking is regional and what you eat depends on where you live and on what happens to be available locally at any particular time.

To visit a market in Italy is to experience what Italian food is all about. Whether it is the famous fish markets of Venice or a small market in a village in the south, the colour and aromas are matched only by the noise. Italian fruit and vegetables are full of colour and flavour; superb aubergines, peppers, tomatoes, peaches, grapes and nectarines make the markets as exciting visually as some of the national monuments.

Pasta is probably associated with Italy more than any other dish. It is alleged to have been brought back from China by Marco Polo in the 13th century. The term 'pasta' can include polentas, gnocchi and rice dishes as well as numerous varieties of stuffed, round, flat, long and short pasta, made with or without eggs. When cooking pasta it is important to use a large quantity of boiling salted water and to cook it only until it is al dente or retaining some firmness. It should be drained as soon as it is cooked. The sauce can be added before serving or served separately, according to taste.

Olive oil is used extensively in the south but in the north it is replaced by butter. Meat is better in the more prosperous north. Veal is the most common meat although Florence has good beef and Umbria is famous for its pork. It is usual for most organs of the animal to be eaten.

Italy also produces a variety of excellent cheeses. Most of the better known are exported and are readily available in stores stocking continental foods.

Vineyards stretch from Verona in the north to Amalfi in the south and produce excellent wines, used liberally in cooking as well as for drinking.

MINESTRONE

Minestrone is undoubtedly the best known of all Italian soups, although there are many regional variations. The following recipe is from Milan.

125 g butter
1 onion, peeled and chopped
125 g diced pickled pork or diced bacon
1 carrot, peeled and chopped
2 sticks celery, chopped
2 zucchini, chopped
¼ small cabbage, finely shredded
250 g dried haricot beans (soaked overnight in cold water)
2 potatoes, peeled and chopped
2½ litres beef stock
1 cup uncooked rice
3 sprigs parsley, chopped
2 cloves garlic, peeled and chopped
small sprig fresh basil or 1 pinch of dried basil
sprig fresh thyme or 1 pinch of dried thyme
⅓ cup Parmesan cheese

Serves 6–8

Melt the butter in a large pan and sauté the onion and pickled pork for 5 minutes. Add the carrot, celery, zucchini, cabbage and beans, cover and cook gently for 15 minutes, stirring occasionally. Add the potatoes and stock, bring to the boil, cover and simmer for 1½ hours. If the soup becomes too thick, pour in a little more water or stock. Add the rice and continue simmering until it is cooked (about 15 minutes). Add the parsley, garlic, basil and thyme, and season with salt and pepper. Stir in the Parmesan and serve, handing around another bowl of grated Parmesan with the soup.

A couple of tablespoons of pesto (see page 70) stirred into the minestrone just before serving makes an excellent addition.

PROSCIUTTO DI PARMA E MELONE

*This simple dish can be made with figs (*fichi*) or pears (*pere*) as well as melon and is ideal for lunch or as a starter to an evening meal. Prosciutto is the Italian word for ham and the best prosciutto comes from the hills around Parma. Here the pigs are specially fed and the stable, airy climate has made possible the perfection of drying and curing techniques, resulting in a ham of unique and delicate flavour. Prosciutto is bought sliced and is best used the same day.*

400 g prosciutto
1 melon (or 8 fresh figs or 4 pears)

Serves 4

Try and buy prosciutto which has been sliced as thinly as possible. Arrange it on individual plates with the slices of melon (or the figs or pears).

GNOCCHI ALLA PARMIGIANA

2½ cups cooked mashed potatoes
2 eggs, beaten
salt and freshly ground pepper

Put the mashed potatoes and eggs in a bowl, season with salt and pepper and mix thoroughly. Add 1½ cups of the flour, stirring well. Place the dough on a floured board and add the rest of the flour.

2¼ cups plain flour
tomato sauce (see below)
grated Parmesan cheese

Serves 4–6

Knead the dough for 3 to 4 minutes. Watch to see the dough does not become too sticky. If this happens sprinkle more flour onto the board. Break the dough into six pieces. Roll out each piece into long sausage-like strips and cut into 2-cm lengths and sprinkle with flour.

Cook the dough by dropping it into a large pan of boiling salted water. When the gnocchi rise to the top they are cooked. Remove with a slotted spoon, drain and keep hot while cooking the remainder. Serve with Italian tomato sauce and sprinkle with the Parmesan.

SALSA DI POMODORO   TOMATO SAUCE

⅓ cup olive oil
2 cloves garlic, peeled and crushed
125 g bacon, finely chopped
400 g canned tomatoes
2 tablespoons tomato paste, diluted in ½ cup hot water
2 sprigs fresh parsley, finely chopped
small sprig fresh basil or ¼ teaspoon dried basil
½ teaspoon sugar
salt and freshly ground pepper

Heat the oil and sauté the garlic. Add the bacon and brown it, stirring occasionally. Add the rest of the ingredients and simmer gently for 45 minutes. Check the seasoning and serve.

LASAGNE PASTICCIATE   BAKED LASAGNA WITH MEAT AND CREAM SAUCES

Many variations exist in lasagna recipes. The squares of pasta used can be home made, bought in packets at supermarkets, or acquired from speciality shops stocking freshly made pasta.

lasagna sheets, packaged or home made

Ragù Bolognese   (Meat Sauce)
2 tablespoons oil
1 onion, peeled and finely chopped
1 clove garlic, peeled and crushed
1 carrot, scraped and finely diced
1 stick celery, finely diced
500 g lean minced beef
2 rashers bacon, chopped
salt and freshly ground black pepper
2 tablespoons tomato purée
1 glass white wine
½ cup beef stock
grated Parmesan
grated nutmeg

Salsa Besciamella   (Béchamel or White Sauce)
1 tablespoon butter
1 tablespoon plain flour
2 cups milk
pinch of salt

Serves 4–6

To make the meat sauce, heat the oil and sauté the chopped vegetables until soft. Add the meat and bacon and cook, stirring until browned (about 10 minutes). Season to taste. Add the tomato purée, wine and stock and stir to mix. Cover and simmer gently for about 45 minutes. The sauce should be thick. Allow to stand while preparing the salsa besciamella.

To make the white sauce melt the butter over a gentle heat and stir in the flour with a wooden spoon. Continue to cook, stirring for about 2 minutes. Do not allow it to burn. Remove from the heat and pour in the milk, stirring as you do so. Return to the heat and stir until boiling. Allow to boil for a minute.

If packaged lasagna is used follow the cooking instructions on the packet. If fresh lasagna is used, cook the required number of sheets, a few at a time, in a large pan of lightly salted boiling water for about 5 minutes. Remove and drain. The number of sheets needed will depend on the size of the casserole used for cooking.

To assemble the lasagne pasticciate, choose a large ovenproof pan and butter it lightly. Cover the bottom with a thin layer of the meat sauce. Spoon over a layer of the white sauce. Sprinkle with a little freshly grated nutmeg and with about 2 tablespoons of grated Parmesan cheese. Arrange a layer of the prepared pasta over the sauces, allowing the ends to turn up the sides of the pan. Repeat this process until the dish is full. The final layer should be one of white sauce. Dust the top with a generous layer of cheese and sprinkle with nutmeg. Bake in a moderate oven for about 45 minutes or until the top is golden.

OSSO BUCO ALLA MILANESE

VEAL SHANKS WITH
WINE AND TOMATOES

The most delicious part of osso buco is the marrow. Some Italian restaurants provide special needles for removing this. Ask your butcher to saw up the veal shanks for you.

**3 whole veal shanks, sawn into
    6-cm pieces
plain flour
salt and freshly ground black pepper
⅔ cup olive oil
1 onion, peeled and sliced
2 carrots, diced
1 stick celery, diced
1 bay leaf
1 cup white wine
1 kg ripe tomatoes, skinned and
    chopped, or canned tomatoes
1 tablespoon tomato paste
1 tablespoon sugar
1 tablespoon vinegar
2 tablespoons chopped parsley
2 cloves garlic, peeled and chopped
2 tablespoons grated lemon peel**

Serves 6–8

Preheat the oven to 180°C/350°F.

Coat the veal shanks in the seasoned flour. Heat ½ cup of the olive oil in a large pan and brown the veal shanks on all sides, turning over carefully.

Heat the remaining oil in another pan and sauté the onion, carrots and celery for 5 minutes. Add the bay leaf. Pour in the wine and simmer until it has reduced by half.

In a large earthenware casserole place the shanks, wine, vegetables, tomatoes, tomato paste, sugar and vinegar. Cover and cook in a moderate oven for about 2–2½ hours, or until the meat pulls away easily from the bone. Watch to see that the liquid does not evaporate during cooking (add a little more wine if necessary). Serve sprinkled with the chopped parsley, garlic and lemon peel.

PESTO ALLA GENOVESE

GENOESE BASIL SAUCE

This delicious sauce comes from Genoa. It is most frequently used on spaghetti or other types of pasta, or on baked potatoes. In its city of origin, pesto is often stirred into minestrone soup before serving. Basil has a particular affinity with tomatoes and the addition of a few chopped leaves will do wonders for many tomato dishes.

**60 g fresh basil leaves, stripped from
    their stalks
2 or 3 cloves garlic, peeled
60 g pine nuts
salt
50 g Parmesan cheese, grated
¼ cup olive oil**

Serves 4

Pesto is best made with a pestle and mortar. However, it can be made in a blender or food processor but will not have such an interesting texture.

Pound the basil leaves and the garlic with the pine nuts and a little salt until a crunchy consistency is obtained. Stir in the grated Parmesan and gradually add the olive oil (as for mayonnaise). The finished pesto should have all the ingredients well amalgamated. The sauce can be made beforehand and stored in the refrigerator.

SALTIMBOCCA ALLA ROMANA

VEAL WITH HAM AND SAGE

Italy has some particularly good veal dishes in its cuisine. When preparing saltimbocca it is important to use the best quality veal available.

Cut the prosciutto into slices the same size as the veal pieces. Lay a piece of prosciutto on top of each slice of veal and on top of this put a fresh sage leaf. Roll the veal up and secure it with a toothpick. Melt a little

Ask the butcher to flatten the veal pieces for you, or do it yourself.

12 slices of prosciutto
12 small slices of veal
12 sage leaves
butter
1 glass Marsala

Serves 4

butter in a large pan and brown the veal parcels, turning until they are browned all over. Add a small glass of Marsala to the pan and let it bubble before covering the pan with a lid. Simmer gently until the meat is tender (about 10 minutes). Remove the veal to a serving dish and keep warm. Scrape all the juices from the pan, pour over the meat and serve.

ARANCI CARAMELLIZZATI   CARAMELISED ORANGES

These oranges take on an almost translucent quality, and look splendid piled up on a dessert dish as a table centrepiece.

8 oranges of uniform size
375 g castor sugar
2 cups of water
3 extra oranges

Serves 8

Peel the 8 oranges and remove all traces of the pith. Make a syrup with the sugar and the water, stirring until the sugar has dissolved. When the syrup has thickened slightly, dip the oranges in, turning them over so that the whole orange is coated with the syrup. This process should take about 2–3 minutes per orange. Pile them up on a dessert dish.

Cut the rind from the 3 other oranges with a potato peeler. Slice it into fine strips about the length of a match (scissors can make this process easier). Plunge the strips into a pan of boiling water and boil for 5 minutes. This will rid the rind of its bitter taste. Drain and cook in the syrup until it begins to caramelise. Take care at this point as the syrup will turn to toffee if left for too long. Put a spoonful of the caramelised rind on top of each orange and serve chilled.

BUDINO DI RICOTTA ALLA ROMANA   ROMAN CHEESE PUDDING

250 g fresh ricotta cheese
½ cup sugar
2 egg yolks
3 eggs
pinch of cinnamon
grated rind of 1 lemon
pinch of salt

Serves 6

Preheat the oven to 160°C/325°F.

Beat the ricotta until smooth, add the sugar and mix well. Beat in the yolks and then drop in the whole eggs, one at a time, beating constantly. Add the rest of the ingredients and stir well. Place the mixture in a buttered mould of 1.5-litre capacity. Place the mould in a baking dish of cold water—allow enough water to reach one-third of the way up the mould. Bake in a moderately slow oven for an hour. Serve hot or cold.

ZABAIONE   CUSTARD WITH MARSALA

The thing to remember when making this delicious sweet is not to let it boil or you will have a dish of Marsala-laced scrambled eggs, instead of an elegant dessert!

8 egg yolks
4 teaspoons sugar
4 sherry glasses of Marsala

Serves 4

This dessert is best cooked in a double boiler, but a heatproof bowl sitting in a pan of simmering water is perfectly adequate. Beat the yolks and sugar in a bowl (off the heat) until they are light and frothy. Stir in the Marsala and pour into the double boiler. The water in the base should be simmering. Stir the yolk mixture constantly. It must not be allowed to boil. The zabaione is ready when the mixture coats the back of the spoon. Pour into warmed glasses and serve at once.

PANFORTE DI SIENA
SIENESE NUT CAKE

This Sienese speciality is now exported to many countries, packaged in distinctive octagonal boxes. In Siena it is possible to sample the cake in various forms; many shops have window displays and will cut and sell the amount required.

⅔ cup plain flour, sifted
1½ cups chopped toasted almonds
½ cup chopped toasted hazelnuts
90 g candied orange peel
90 g candied lemon peel
125 g candied pumpkin or melon peel
¼ cup powdered cocoa
pinch of black pepper
4 drops vanilla extract
2½ teaspoons cinnamon
⅓ cup castor sugar
½ cup honey
2 tablespoons icing sugar

Serves 8–10

Preheat the oven to 150°C/300°F and grease a shallow cake tin and line it with waxed paper.

In a large bowl place the flour, almonds, hazelnuts, orange and lemon peel, pumpkin peel, cocoa, pepper, vanilla and 1½ teaspoons of the cinnamon. Mix well.

Melt the castor sugar and honey in a large pan over a gentle heat. Stir constantly with a wooden spoon until a teaspoon of the mixture forms a soft ball when dropped into cold water. Remove from the heat and add the nut mixture. Combine ingredients well and put into the prepared tin, smooth the top and bake in the oven for 35 minutes. Take out of the oven and allow to cool in the tin. Remove the cake and carefully peel off the waxed paper. Sprinkle with the rest of the cinnamon and icing sugar. Wrap in heavy waxed paper and store in a cool place. This cake makes an ideal present and will keep fresh for a couple of months.

GRANITA DI LIMONE
LEMON ICE

Granite are the Italian equivalent of sorbets or water ices. They are simple to prepare and should be grainy in consistency.

1¼ cups lemon juice (6–7 lemons)
125 g sugar
2 cups hot water

Serves 4–6

Squeeze the lemons. Dissolve the sugar in the water and add the lemon juice. Allow to cool and then place in the freezer for about 3 hours. Orange granita can be made in the same way as the lemon variety, but a little less sugar will be required. A squeeze of lemon juice improves the flavour of the orange ice.

GRANITA DI FRAGOLE
STRAWBERRY ICE

1 kg strawberries
juice of 1 orange
juice of ½ lemon
200 g sugar
1¼ cups water

Serves 4–6

Wash and hull the strawberries and purée in a blender. Add the juice of the orange and lemon and place the mixture in an icecream container. Put the sugar and water into a pan and stir over a low heat until the sugar has dissolved. Allow this syrup to cool and then pour into the strawberry purée. Place in the freezer for about 3 hours.

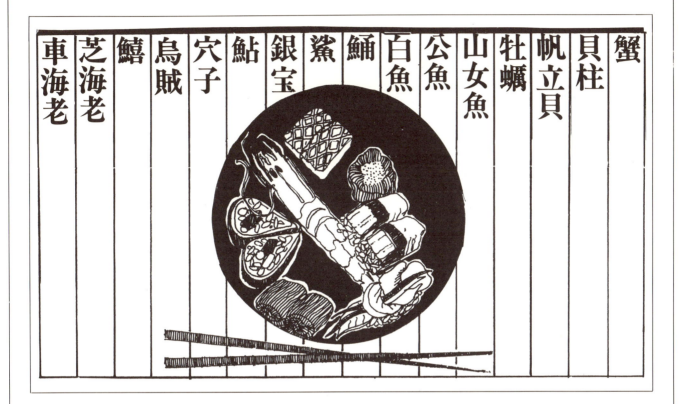

蟹　貝柱　帆立貝　牡蠣　山女魚　公魚　白魚　鰤　鯊　銀宝　鮎　穴子　烏賊　鱚　芝海老　車海老

Japanese food is unique, exciting the eye as well as the palate. Flavours are delicate, the freshness of the ingredients is of prime importance and most noticeable of all, the presentation is exquisite.

Japanese food has been underrated in the past, partly because until recently it has been difficult to obtain the necessary ingredients outside Japan. The opening of some excellent restaurants has stimulated interest in Japanese food and it is probably a good idea to visit one of these before attempting to prepare a Japanese meal yourself.

Like the Chinese, the Japanese traditionally did not use ovens and consequently less time is spent on cooking and the ingredients of a meal tend to retain their original shape and flavour. Much Japanese food is served cold with the best known being perhaps sashimi *or raw fish. A great variety of raw fish is eaten, including* fugu *or blowfish. This latter must be treated with extreme caution because unless cleaned properly, it can cause death by poisoning in only 5 minutes!*

A Japanese meal tends to follow no particular pattern, with many dishes being served together. Soup for example, can be served with the meal or at the end. Sake, slightly warmed, is drunk with the meal from small china cups. The meal concludes with green tea and a bowl of rice and some pickles.

SASHIMI

Sashimi is raw fish, sliced and served on individual platters with a little grated Japanese radish and watercress or seaweed. It is accompanied by a small saucer of Japanese horseradish and soy sauce. It is usually served at the beginning of a meal before the palate has become jaded.

fish (tuna, kingfish, jewfish, snapper, garfish or prawns)
Japanese radish, grated
watercress or seaweed

Sauce
Japanese soy sauce
fresh ginger, grated
hot mustard or lemon juice
Japanese horseradish

The freshness, elegance and simplicity of presentation in Japanese food is typified in sashimi. Only the freshest seafood is suitable and the choosing of this is the most important step in the preparation.

The fish listed opposite are suggestions only. The fish should be cleaned and filleted, sliced finely (prawns, if used, are left whole) and then plunged into iced water for 5 minutes. Remove and drain before arranging on platters. The grated radish and watercress can be placed as a side garnish on the same dishes. Serve with a small bowl containing Japanese soy sauce mixed with a little grated fresh ginger, hot mustard or lemon juice. A little horseradish may be mixed into the dipping sauce, the amount depending on individual taste. The fish is then dipped with chopsticks into the sauce before eating.

SUIMONO

The basis for this soup is dashi (fish stock). It is available in a dried form. Water and a little sugar are added to make the stock. Amounts may be varied according to taste.

6 cups dashi
2 teaspoons Japanese soy sauce
1 teaspoon rice vinegar
salt
tōfu (allow 2–3 bite-sized pieces per person)
3 spring onions, including tops, finely chopped
4 strips fine lemon rind

Serves 4

Bring the dashi to the boil and add the soy sauce and rice vinegar and season with salt. Add the tōfu and heat through. With a slotted spoon carefully remove the tōfu, putting 2–3 pieces in each bowl. Add the spring onions and a length of the lemon rind to each bowl. Ladle the boiling dashi into the bowls and serve at once. In Japan, this soup would be served with the meal or at the end of the meal, not at the beginning as in Western countries.

CHAWAN MUSHI

STEAMED EGG CUSTARD WITH SEAFOOD

1 chicken fillet (about 250 g)
1 tablespoon Japanese soy sauce
8 large prawns, shelled, de-veined and cut into pieces
1 tablespoon sake
6 cups dashi (fish stock) or chicken broth
salt
4 eggs
8 button mushrooms, wiped with a damp cloth, with the bases trimmed and caps sliced

This is basically a baked custard to which pieces of chicken, seafood and vegetables have been added. It is unusual as far as Japanese cuisine goes as it is eaten with a spoon. It is normally served hot, but can be served cold if preferred. The ingredients should all be prepared before the custard.

Preheat the oven to 180°C/350°F.

Finely slice the chicken and chop into pieces no longer than 4 cm. Place in a bowl and sprinkle with the soy sauce and leave to marinate. In a separate dish spatter the prawns with the sake and allow to marinate.

Heat the dashi and season to taste. Beat the eggs, pour the hot dashi over them and mix well.

Drain the chicken and prawns and arrange in the bottom of individual

6 slivers lemon rind
boiling water
1 handful fresh spinach, thoroughly
    washed, drained and torn into pieces,
    or a small bunch of watercress,
    cleaned and chopped

Serves 4–6

ovenproof dishes, together with the mushrooms and lemon rind. Carefully pour the strained custard into the bowls. Stand the bowls in a baking tin and pour in enough boiling water to reach half-way up the sides of the dishes. Bake in a moderate oven for about 20 minutes. Remove from the oven and add the spinach, pressing it down into the custard. Return to the oven and cook until set—it is normal for the custard to retain some liquid.

SUNOMONO

VINEGARED VEGETABLES WITH SEAFOOD

1 Japanese radish
1 carrot
200 g green beans
200 g broccoli
150 g snow peas
200 g scallops
dried bonito flakes for garnishing
    (optional)

Dressing
6 tablespoons rice vinegar
2 tablespoons sugar
2 teaspoons Japanese soy sauce
pinch of salt

Serves 4

To make the dressing, mix all the ingredients together in a bowl and leave to stand while preparing the vegetables and seafood.

Grate the radish and carrot. Top and tail the beans and lightly steam them. Also steam the broccoli and the snow peas. It is important that all the vegetables retain their crispness. Plunge them into a bowl of iced water after they have been steamed. Gently poach the scallops and slice them.

Allow one small bowl per person and fill with the prepared vegetables and seafood. Spoon a little of the dressing over the contents of each bowl. Dried bonito flakes can be sprinkled over this dish as a garnish to give added texture and flavour.

TEMPURA

DEEP FRIED SEAFOOD AND VEGETABLES

8 large prawns
1 aubergine
2 zucchini
small head of broccoli per person
8 mushrooms
corn oil for frying

Batter
1 egg, beaten
$\frac{3}{4}$ cup plain flour
$\frac{1}{4}$ cup cornflour
$\frac{3}{4}$–1 cup iced water or soda water

Sauce
1$\frac{1}{4}$ cups dashi (fish stock)
$\frac{1}{4}$ cup mirin or sweet sherry
$\frac{1}{4}$ cup Japanese soy sauce
pinch of monosodium glutamate

Serves 4

The ingredients used in tempura depend upon individual tastes. However, it is usual to have some type of seafood and the vegetables can include zucchini, mushrooms, carrot, aubergine, broccoli, pumpkin, etc. At least four different types of vegetables should be served. The batter must be light and the oil used for cooking must be kept at a consistent heat.

Shell and de-vein the prawns, retaining the tails. Cut the aubergine into pieces about 6 cm by 2 cm. Slice the zucchini into uniform pieces and halve the mushrooms.

To make the sauce, bring the stock, mirin and soy sauce to the boil. Add the monosodium glutamate. Pour into individual bowls.

The batter must be made just before it is to be used and should be of a thin consistency. Add the water or soda water to the beaten egg and beat until light. Sift the flours together and add to the egg mixture. Working quickly, mix together, but do not overmix. Thin the batter by adding more water if necessary.

Heat about 8 cm of corn oil in a heavy based pan. Dip the prepared seafood and vegetables into the batter, shake off the surplus and fry in the hot oil until golden. The batter should be crisp and light when cooked. Drain and serve accompanied by a small bowl of sauce per person.

If desired, tempura can be served as a main course. It is best to arrange the prepared seafood and vegetables on a platter and have the batter and oil, kept hot over a gas ring, in the centre of the table. Each person then dips and cooks their own tempura.

SUSHI

VINEGARED RICE WITH RAW SEAFOOD AND VEGETABLES

1 cup short-grain rice
soy sauce for dipping

Vinegar
4 tablespoons rice vinegar
4 tablespoons sugar
2 teaspoons salt

Suggested Toppings
fillets of raw fish, finely sliced (tuna, bream, prawns, etc.)
fresh ginger, chopped
cucumber, chopped
Japanese radish, grated
horseradish
seaweed

Omelette
2 eggs
1 teaspoon sugar
pinch of salt
oil for frying

Serves 4

Sushi is a combination of vinegared rice, raw seafood and vegetables, is often rolled in seaweed or strips of Japanese omelette, and is served as a full meal. Long, narrow sushi bars abound in Japan. The raw fish used in the dish is displayed in a glass case on top of a wooden counter which runs along one side of the bar and the vinegared rice is kept in a large wooden tub. The customer indicates his choice of topping and the sushi is expertly constructed before his eyes.

Cook the rice until it is sticky. Heat the ingredients for the vinegar, stirring until the sugar is dissolved and add to the rice while still warm. In Japan the rice is fanned until it reaches room temperature.

To make the omelette, mix the eggs in a bowl with chopsticks, add the sugar and salt and stir. Lightly grease an omelette pan and heat. Pour half the egg mixture into the pan, tilting to cover the base thinly. Cook over a gentle heat until the surface of the omelette is almost dry. Carefully turn and cook the other side. Remove and allow to cool. Repeat this procedure with the rest of the mixture. Cut the omelette into 3-cm strips.

To prepare the sushi, mould the rice with wet hands into ovals about 3 cm long and flatten the top. If desired the sides of the moulded rice may be wrapped in seaweed (available in Asian groceries) or a strip of omelette before garnishing. Sprinkle the sushi with a little horseradish or ginger, top with a piece of raw fish and garnish with slivers of a fresh vegetable. Serve accompanied by a bowl of soy sauce and eat either with chopsticks or with the fingers.

TORI TERIYAKI

MARINATED CHICKEN

500 g chicken fillets
2 tablespoons sesame seeds, toasted
2 tablespoons oil for frying

Marinade
¼ cup sake
¼ cup mirin or sweet sherry
½ cup Japanese soy sauce
2 cloves garlic, peeled and crushed
2 teaspoons fresh ginger, finely chopped
½ teaspoon brown sugar

Serves 4

Cut the chicken into bite-sized pieces. Place the ingredients for the marinade in a bowl and marinate the chicken for at least 2 hours. Drain the chicken. Heat the oil in a heavy based pan and cook the chicken for about 5 minutes over a moderate heat. Place the sesame seeds in a small pan over a low heat and cook until golden. Sprinkle the chicken with the sesame seeds and serve.

SUKIYAKI

LIGHTLY COOKED BEEF AND VEGETABLES

180 g Japanese noodles or vermicelli
500 g fillet steak, cut into bite-sized wafer-thin slices

Sukiyaki is cooked at the table which enables people to help themselves directly from the cooking pan and eliminates the possibility of the food being overcooked. A gas ring is best for this method of cooking and it

1 small bunch spring onions, including
   tops, cut into 5-cm lengths
250 g button mushrooms
2 sticks celery, sliced into 5-cm
   diagonal pieces
250 g Chinese cabbage, sliced
1 small can bamboo shoots, sliced
1 piece tōfu (about 150 g), cut into
   chunks
small piece suet

Sauce
$\frac{1}{2}$ cup dashi (fish stock)
$\frac{1}{2}$ cup Japanese soy sauce
4 tablespoons sugar
$\frac{1}{4}$ cup mirin or sweet sherry

Serving Suggestions
4 small bowls cooked rice, hot
4 eggs

Serves 4

is important that a constant source of heat is maintained. The preparation and presentation of the ingredients is important. All the food must be carefully sliced and arranged on a large platter in a way that looks appetising. Use prime quality beef for sukiyaki—the other ingredients may be varied to suit individual tastes.

Cook the noodles in boiling salted water and drain. When they are cool arrange them with the other ingredients (except the suet) on a large platter.

To make the sauce combine all the ingredients together and pour into four small dishes.

Break the eggs into four small bowls. Place a bowl of hot rice, a bowl of egg and a dish of sauce in front of each table setting. Each person can beat their egg by whisking with chopsticks.

Heat a pan in the centre of the table and rub it with the suet. Add some of the sliced beef, turning it with chopsticks so that it browns evenly. Add a little of the sauce and a selection of the other ingredients. As the food is cooked, remove it with chopsticks, dip it into the beaten egg and then into the rice bowl before eating. Replenish the food as it is eaten and top up the sauce from time to time. The food must not be overcooked: the beef will be tough if it is left on the heat too long and the vegetables will lose their bite and colour.

At the end of the meal the cooking liquid is served as a soup in small bowls. In Japan sukiyaki would be followed by fresh fruit, cut and arranged on a platter, and accompanied by cups of green tea.

NASU KUSHI-YAKI
SKEWERS OF AUBERGINE

3 aubergines (the thin variety)
salt
2 tablespoons sesame oil
2 tablespoons vegetable oil
white sesame seeds for garnishing

Sauce
6 tablespoons miso paste
3 tablespoons mirin or sweet sherry
1 tablespoon sugar

Serves 4–6

Cut the aubergines into bite-sized pieces, stand in a colander and sprinkle with salt. Allow to stand for $\frac{1}{2}$ an hour and then rinse under a cold tap. This will draw out the bitterness. Pat dry and thread the pieces on to bamboo skewers.

Mix the two oils and brush the skewered aubergine. Grill lightly. Mix together the miso paste, mirin and sugar. Remove the skewers from the grill and brush the aubergine with this sauce. Return to the grill and cook until the aubergine is tender. Remove from the grill and brush once again with the sauce. Sprinkle with sesame seeds and serve at once accompanied by the rest of the sauce.

NARAZUKE
PICKLED MELON

1 medium-sized cantaloupe or honey
   dew melon
pinch of salt
$\frac{1}{4}$ cup brandy
$\frac{3}{4}$ cup sherry

Serves 4

You will need to prepare this dish 5 days before it is required. Peel the melon, remove the seeds and slice. Place in a bowl, sprinkle with salt and pour over the brandy and sherry. Cover and allow to stand for 5 days. Drain off the liquid. Serve the melon at the end of the meal.

Mexican food is based on three staples: tortillas, Mexican bread made from maize flour; beans, a major source of protein; and taco fillings and sauces. Much of the cuisine is derived from that of the Mayas and Aztecs. When the Spaniards arrived in Mexico in 1519, they found not only abundant gold and silver but many plants and animals previously unknown to Europeans such as cocoa, maize, peanuts, peppers, potatoes, tomatoes, vanilla and turkeys.

About 150 varieties of peppers are grown in Mexico, varying enormously in appearance and taste, ranging from sweet to searingly hot. Chillies are very popular; the green ones are used fresh, and those that have ripened to red are generally dried.

Breakfast is an important meal for Mexicans and may be eaten at a café. It might begin with fresh orange juice and a platter of fresh fruit, over which lime juice is squeezed. One of a number of dishes combining eggs, tomatoes, beans and chillies may come next and the meal is finished with coffee or hot chocolate.

Snacks are eaten at any time while lunch, the main meal of the day, is served between 1 p.m. and 4 p.m. A typical lunch starts with a small basket of tortillas and a dish of guacamole (an avocado dip), followed by a chicken-based soup, a dish of fish or meat and a dessert or fresh fruit. The evening meal is not eaten until after 8 p.m. and usually consists of only one dish such as an omelette.

SOPA DE AGUACATE

AVOCADO SOUP

This is a smooth and subtle soup and is ideal as a starter if you are serving spicy dishes.

4 tablespoons butter
3 tablespoons plain flour
7 cups chicken stock
3 large ripe avocados
½ small onion, peeled and grated
½ cup cream
salt and freshly ground black pepper
coriander or parsley for garnishing

Serves 6

In a large pan melt the butter, stir in the flour and cook for 2 minutes, stirring constantly with a wooden spoon. Do not allow the mixture to brown. Remove the pan from the heat and stir in the stock, slowly at first. When the stock is thoroughly blended, return to the stove and cook, stirring until it boils. Allow the stock to cool slightly.

Peel, seed and chop the avocados. Retain the seeds. Place one cup of the stock in the blender with the chopped avocados, and blend until smooth. Slowly add the avocado mixture to the stock in the pan, stirring constantly. Add the grated onion, half the cream, and season to taste. Continue stirring and heat to blend the flavours.

It is best to make this soup just before it is to be served as avocados become grey if left to stand. If you wish to leave it for several hours, place the whole seeds in the soup—this will help it to keep its colour. Remove the seeds before serving. Serve hot or cold, spoon the remaining cream into the soup and garnish with a sprig of coriander or parsley.

GUACAMOLE

AVOCADO DIP

2 ripe avocados
3 cloves garlic, peeled and crushed
juice of 1 lemon
2 tomatoes, peeled, seeded and coarsely
  chopped
1 medium onion, peeled and grated
1 tablespoon coriander or parsley, finely
  chopped
3 tablespoons olive oil
salt and freshly ground black pepper
dash of Tabasco

Peel and mash the avocados. Add the garlic, lemon juice, tomatoes, onion, coriander and olive oil. Season with salt and pepper and add a dash of Tabasco to taste. If you are not eating the guacamole immediately put it into a bowl and press the avocado seed down into the middle of the dip to prevent it from turning brown. Cover with plastic wrap and refrigerate.

CEVICHE ESTILO ACAPULCO

RAW FISH MARINATED IN
ACAPULCO STYLE

500 g scallops or fish suitable for
  marinating and eating raw
juice of 4 limes or lemons
250 g tomatoes, peeled, seeded and
  chopped
2 fresh chillies, seeded and finely
  chopped
4 tablespoons olive oil
1 tablespoon wine vinegar
3 tablespoons coriander or parsley,
  chopped
salt and freshly ground black pepper
1 red onion, sliced

Serves 4–6

This dish makes a light and tangy appetiser or an ideal luncheon dish. Among the fish that are suitable for use are trumpeter, tuna, jewfish and snapper. The fish should be extremely fresh and should be cleaned and filleted then plunged into iced water for 5 minutes before being drained and sliced for use.

Cut the seafood into small pieces, place in a glass bowl and pour the lime juice over the top. Allow to stand for about 5 hours in a cool place or in the refrigerator, stirring from time to time.

Just before serving, remove the excess lime juice, add the tomatoes, chillies, olive oil, vinegar, coriander or parsley and season with salt and pepper. Stir carefully to mix well. Garnish with thin slices of the red onion.

HUEVOS RANCHEROS

COUNTRY-STYLE EGGS

$\frac{1}{2}$ cup oil
1 small onion, peeled and finely
    chopped
1 clove garlic, peeled and crushed
2 cups tomatoes, puréed
1 small chilli, seeded and finely
    chopped
salt and freshly ground black pepper
8 eggs
4 tortillas
2 avocados
1 tablespoon chopped parsley

Serves 4

Heat 1 tablespoon of the oil in a pan and cook the onion and garlic until soft. Add the puréed tomatoes and chilli and simmer until the sauce thickens slightly. Season to taste and keep warm.

Heat half the remaining oil in another pan and fry the eggs, being careful not to break the yolks. When cooked, carefully remove them to a warm plate and cover. Heat the rest of the oil in the same pan. When it is almost smoking cook the tortillas until soft but do not allow them to get brown. Drain the tortillas on kitchen paper and place them on four heated plates. Top each one with two fried eggs, and spoon the warm sauce over the eggs. Garnish with the sliced avocado and chopped parsley.

TORTILLAS

FLAT PANCAKES

Tortillas are flat pancakes that are made with maize flour, water and salt. They come from the Aztec cuisine and are one of the staples of the Mexican diet, forming the basis for Mexico's best loved foods, the enchilada and the taco. An enchilada is a tortilla that has been stuffed with a spicy filling, rolled up like a crepe, covered with a sauce and baked in the oven. The taco is a tortilla which has been folded in half and fried until crisp, then stuffed with a combination of meat, lettuce, tomato and topped with a spicy sauce. (See below for salsa de chile rojo, a red chilli sauce which can be used in tortillas, enchiladas or tacos.)

2 cups masa harina (maize flour), sifted
1 teaspoon salt
1$\frac{1}{4}$ cups warm water

Makes 15 tortillas

Place the flour and salt in a bowl, add the water and mix until a dough is formed. It should not be too sticky. Leave to stand for $\frac{1}{2}$ an hour. Break the dough into about 15 pieces and roll each portion into a ball. Tortillas were originally shaped by placing the dough between the palms of the hands and patting it until flat. This is still the best way, but if you wish they can be rolled between two sheets of waxed paper. They should be about †5 cm in diameter.

Heat a heavy based frying pan but do not grease it. Cook the tortillas for about 2 minutes on each side. They should be lightly flecked with brown spots.

SALSA DE CHILE ROJO

RED CHILLI SAUCE

$\frac{1}{4}$ cup vegetable oil
1 onion, peeled and chopped
2 cloves garlic, peeled and crushed
5 small dried red chillies
3 tablespoons boiling water
400 g canned tomatoes
2 tablespoons tomato paste
1 teaspoon ground cummin
2 tablespoons wine vinegar
1 teaspoon sugar

Serves 4–6

Chillies are used extensively in Mexican cooking and vary in type from hot to fiery. You will have to experiment in order to ascertain how much chilli you should use for your own individual taste. This particular sauce can be used with meat or poultry, as an accompaniment to tortillas, tacos or enchiladas.

Heat the oil and sauté the onion and garlic until soft. Place the cooked onion and garlic in a blender with all the other ingredients and blend until smooth. Return the sauce to the pan, cover and simmer for 10–15 minutes. If the sauce is not to be used immediately, cover and refrigerate until required.

MEXICO: A selection of fruits and vegetables.

POLLO EN CEBOLLA
CHICKEN WITH ONIONS AND NUTMEG

6 tablespoons oil
2 medium-sized chickens cut into
  serving pieces
5 onions, peeled and chopped
3 cloves garlic, peeled and chopped
4–5 cups water
3 sprigs fresh thyme or 1 teaspoon
  dried thyme
2 bay leaves
3 sprigs coriander or parsley
salt and freshly ground black pepper
1 whole nutmeg
coriander or parsley for garnishing

Serves 6

This dish can be made in advance and reheated on the day of use.

In a large pan or electric frying pan heat the oil and brown the chicken, turning until all sides are browned. Remove from the pan and cook the onion and garlic in the same oil, stirring until golden brown. Return the chicken to the pan, pour in the water until the chicken is just covered and add the thyme, bay leaves and parsley. Season with salt and pepper and grate the whole nutmeg over the chicken. Cover the pan and simmer very slowly until the chicken is very tender and the sauce is dark and rich. Garnish with coriander or parsley and serve.

FRIJOLES REFRITOS
REFRIED BEANS

2 cups red kidney beans
2 onions, peeled and finely chopped
2 cloves garlic, peeled
1 bay leaf
2 sprigs coriander or parsley
2 small chillies
salt and freshly ground black pepper
$\frac{1}{3}$ cup bacon fat
1 tomato, peeled, seeded and chopped

Serves 4

Rinse the beans under running water, place in a medium-sized saucepan and add 1 of the onions, 1 garlic clove, the herbs and chillies. Cover with cold water, bring to the boil, reduce the heat and simmer, adding more water if necessary. Simmer until the beans are soft, season with salt and pepper and cook for another 30 minutes. There should not be much liquid remaining at this stage.

Heat the bacon fat in a pan and sauté the remaining onion and garlic until soft, add the tomato and cook for another couple of minutes. Remove the pan from the heat and add a few spoonfuls of the beans together with some of their remaining liquid. Mash the mixture until it forms a smooth paste. Continue to add beans and liquid, working to achieve the smooth paste after each addition. Check and adjust the seasoning if necessary—the beans should have a bland flavour. They are ready when the paste has become dry. This is especially good served with huevos rancheros (see page 80).

BUDIN DE CALABACITAS
ZUCCHINI PUDDING

750 g zucchini
salt
1 tablespoon oil
250 g tomatoes, peeled and seeded
2 dried red chillies, seeded and cut into
  fine strips
salt and freshly ground black pepper
2 egg yolks
$\frac{1}{4}$ cup cream
2 egg whites
125 g ricotta cheese, cut into slices
1 cup sour cream

Serves 4

Preheat the oven to 180°C/350°F and grease a 2-litre ovenproof dish.

Shred the zucchini into a colander, sprinkle with salt and allow to stand for 1 hour. Using your hands squeeze all the excess moisture from the zucchini.

Heat the oil in a heavy pan and cook the tomatoes and chillies for about 5 minutes while stirring. Season to taste. Remove from the heat and allow to cool to room temperature. In a bowl beat the egg yolks until light and frothy and add to the zucchini along with the cream and the tomato mixture. Mix well. Whisk the egg whites until stiff and fold into the zucchini mixture. Adjust the seasoning if necessary.

Pour the zucchini mixture into the prepared dish and bake in the oven until set—about $\frac{1}{2}$ an hour. Place the sliced cheese over the top and return to the oven just long enough for the cheese to melt slightly. Serve accompanied by the sour cream which should be spooned over the pudding before eating.

PORTUGAL: Limões Recheados com Sardinhas (Lemons Stuffed with Sardines). See page 88.

FLAN DE NARANJA

ORANGE FLAN

The flan is the dessert most commonly found in Mexico and is similar to what we know as a creme caramel. While there are variations using coconut, nuts, etc., the following is made with freshly squeezed orange juice.

¾ cup castor sugar
3 eggs
1 egg yolk
2 cups freshly squeezed orange juice, strained
1 tablespoon cornflour
2 tablespoons water
1 teaspoon orange rind, finely grated

Serves 4

Preheat the oven to 160°C/320°F and grease an ovenproof flan dish (preferably one with a lid).

Put ½ cup of the sugar in a pan with a heavy base and cook over a high heat, stirring constantly with a wooden spoon until the sugar turns a deep golden brown. Take care not to let it burn. As soon as the caramel is ready, pour it into the prepared flan dish and swirl it around to coat the base.

Beat the eggs and yolk together until the mixture is thick and light. Mix the remaining ¼ cup of sugar into the orange juice and stir to dissolve. Mix the cornflour with the water and add to the orange juice. Add the orange juice mixture to the beaten eggs along with the grated orange rind, stirring well. Pour the mixture into the prepared dish and cover with the lid (if the flan dish does not have a lid, use aluminium foil to make an airtight cover). Place in a pan of cold water (the water should come half-way up the sides of the flan dish). Cook in the preheated oven for 1½ hours or until set. When cool, carefully run a knife around the edge and invert the flan on to a serving plate with the caramel side up.

DULCE DE PAPAYA

PAPAW PASTE

4 small green papaws
2 cups dark brown sugar
juice of ½ lemon
cream for serving

Serves 4

Cut the papaws in half and remove the seeds. Leave the skins on. Steam the fruit until it is tender. Place the brown sugar in a large pan with a heavy base, add the lemon juice and a little water and cook stirring over a gentle heat until a syrup forms.

Scoop the papaw from its skin and mash it. Add the fruit to the syrup in the pan and stir over a gentle heat until the mixture forms a thick paste. It is not necessary to stir constantly, but make sure it does not burn. This dessert can be served hot or cold with cream.

CHONGOS ZAMORANOS

CINNAMON CUSTARD

This dessert is similar to a custard. The egg yolks can be omitted if desired.

6 cups milk
3 eggs yolks, beaten
2 rennet tablets
2 tablespoons warm water
1 cup sugar
1 cinnamon stick, lightly crushed

Serves 6

Warm the milk slightly and mix the beaten egg yolks into it. Dissolve the rennet in the warm water and add to the egg mixture. Place in a heatproof dish and stand in a pan of hot water for about 30 minutes or until the milk mixture has started to set. Cut into six portions and sprinkle with the sugar and the cinnamon stick. Place the heatproof dish (still in the pan of water) over a very low heat and simmer until the liquid (whey) and the sugar have formed a light syrup. This may take up to 2 hours. Serve at room temperature.

Poland once boasted an aristocracy which enjoyed a grand and sumptuous life-style. Today, however, the majority of Poles are farmers who supplement their diet with wild game killed in the hunting season and fish caught from the streams which criss-cross the country.

Perhaps owing to the rigorous climate, Polish food is hearty and warming. Bigos is a national dish made during the hunting season from game, meat, sausages and sauerkraut. Soups are filling and provide an excellent source of nourishment during the long Polish winter and are economical to make. Barszcz is a soup made from dried mushrooms and traditionally is served on Christmas Eve and during Easter. Pork is the cheapest and most plentiful meat and is smoked for ham and made into delicious sausages, while poultry is mostly free-range and full of flavour.

Dumplings are prepared with fillings of cabbage or mushrooms while tripe is made into soup or cooked with vegetables. Both savoury and sweet pancakes come filled with many interesting combinations and are sometimes served with sour cream. Cucumber prepared with herbs accompanies many meals as do gherkins and horseradish.

Vodka, originally distilled by the monasteries for medicinal purposes, is now a popular aperitif when served with ice and lemon and accompanied by cheese or nuts. Another popular drink is a liqueur made from excellent Polish honey and is served with strong black coffee.

BARSZCZ

250 g dried mushrooms
3 carrots, peeled and chopped
3 onions, peeled and chopped
2 sticks celery, including tops, chopped
1 teaspoon white vinegar
1 litre water
salt and freshly ground black pepper
1 cup macaroni
$\frac{1}{4}$ cup cream

Serves 4

You should begin preparing this soup the day before it is required. Soak the mushrooms in cold water overnight. The next day, put the prepared vegetables in a pan with the drained mushrooms, vinegar and water. Bring to the boil and simmer for 30 minutes. Season with salt and pepper, add the macaroni and simmer for about 15 minutes or until the pasta is cooked. Remove from the heat, stir in the cream and serve.

PIROZHKIS

250 g salmon, fresh or tinned
$\frac{1}{4}$ cup cream
1 tablespoon parsley, finely chopped
salt and freshly ground black pepper
shortcrust pastry (see page 31)
oil for frying
1 lemon, quartered

Serves 4

Remove any skin and bones from the salmon and mash it with a fork. Add the cream and parsley, season with salt and pepper and mix well. Roll out the pastry on a floured board and cut it into rounds about the size of a teacup.

Place spoonfuls of the salmon mixture in the centre of each pastry round, cover with another round and pinch the edges together firmly so that none of the filling is lost during cooking. Heat some oil until smoking and deep fry the pirozhkis a few at a time until golden. Drain on absorbent paper and serve with pieces of lemon.

FLAKI PO POLSKU

1 kg tripe
1 carrot
1 onion
2 sticks celery
3 tablespoons butter
3 tablespoons plain flour
6 cups white stock
2 sprigs parsley
1 teaspoon dried marjoram
$\frac{1}{2}$ teaspoon ground ginger
salt and freshly ground black pepper
grated cheese for serving

Serves 6

An authentic tripe dish can take up to 12 hours to cook. Thankfully most butchers sell tripe already prepared and partly cooked. Cut the tripe into 4-cm lengths. Peel and chop the carrot, onion and celery. Melt the butter, stir in the flour and gradually add the stock, stirring all the time. Add the vegetables, tripe, herbs and ginger to the stock. Season to taste with salt and pepper. Cover and simmer for 45 minutes to 1 hour or until the tripe is tender. Serve with grated cheese.

BIGOS

250 g dried mushrooms
500 g hare
250 g lamb
250 g beef

You will need to start preparing this dish two days before it is required. Soak the mushrooms overnight. The next day cut all the meat (except the sausages and bacon) into bite-sized pieces. Heat the oil in a large pan and brown the meat. Add the mushrooms together with the liquid they

250 g pork
oil for cooking
1 tablespoon plain flour
salt and freshly ground black pepper
1 kg sauerkraut
250 g pork sausages
8 rashers bacon, chopped
1¼ cups Madeira

Serves 6–8

have been soaking in. Stir in the flour, season with salt and pepper and add the sauerkraut. Pour in enough water to cover the contents of the pan and simmer over a low heat for 2 hours. Allow to stand overnight.

They next day add the sausages and the bacon. Simmer gently for an hour, add the Madeira and stir. Cook for another 10 minutes and serve.

GOLNKA KASZONA KAPUSTA   HAM HOCKS AND SAUERKRAUT

4 large ham hocks
1 bay leaf
3 cups sauerkraut
1 onion, peeled and sliced
1 tablespoon sugar
freshly ground black pepper
boiled potatoes for serving

Serves 4

Put the hocks in a large pot with the bay leaf, cover with water and simmer for 1 hour. Drain. Put the sauerkraut, onion and sugar in with the hocks, season with pepper, cover and return to the heat. Simmer for about 1½ hours or until the ham is falling off the bone. Serve with boiled potatoes.

SZTINAK SALATKA   RAW SPINACH SALAD

250 g fresh spinach, thoroughly washed
    and dried
1 small green pepper, seeded and
    chopped
1 small onion, peeled and cut into rings
2 tablespoons salad oil
1 tablespoon lemon juice
salt and freshly ground black pepper
3 hardboiled eggs, halved
1 small can anchovies

Serves 6

Tear the spinach leaves into bite-sized pieces, discarding the stems. Put the spinach into a large salad bowl and add the green pepper and onion rings.

Make a dressing with the oil and lemon juice and season with salt and freshly ground pepper. Pour the dressing over the salad and toss. Serve garnished with the halved hardboiled eggs and the anchovies.

WARSZAWSKA SALATKA   WARSAW SALAD

1 large continental cucumber
6 large radishes
2 Granny Smith apples
½ cup sour cream
2 tablespoons lemon juice
salt and freshly ground black pepper
2 tablespoons parsley, finely chopped

Serves 4

Slice the cucumber paper thin. Wash and thinly slice the radishes. Wash, core and slice the apples. Combine the cucumber, radishes and apple in a bowl and mix. Combine the sour cream and lemon juice and pour over the salad. Season with salt and pepper and garnish with the parsley.

NALEŚNIKI Z SEREM

PANCAKES WITH COTTAGE CHEESE

1 teaspoon castor sugar
1 cup milk
2 eggs, beaten
¾ cup plain flour
½ teaspoon vanilla
1½ tablespoons melted butter
butter for cooking
icing sugar for serving

Filling
¾ cup cottage cheese
1 egg yolk
½ teaspoon cinnamon
1 teaspoon lemon rind, finely grated
2 teaspoons castor sugar
½ teaspoon vanilla
2 tablespoons kirsch

Serves 6

Mix the sugar and milk into the beaten eggs. Fold in the flour. Add the vanilla and melted butter. Beat until smooth (the batter should be fairly thin) and allow to stand for ½ an hour. This batter will make six pancakes.

While the batter is standing, make the filling. Blend the cottage cheese until it is smooth. Add the other ingredients and stir to mix.

Grease a heavy based pan and heat. Pour in enough batter to coat the base. Cook until bubbles appear and the underneath is brown. Turn the pancake and cook until the other side is brown. Stack the pancakes on a warm plate while cooking the rest of the batter. Spoon the filling on to each warm pancake. Roll them up and serve dusted with icing sugar.

SERNIK

CHEESE CAKE

rich shortcrust pastry (see page 133)

Filling
3 egg yolks
4 tablespoons castor sugar
500 g cottage cheese
1 tablespoon cornflour
½ teaspoon vanilla essence
1 cup sour cream
2 tablespoons sultanas
3 egg whites

Serves 8–10

Preheat the oven to 180°C/350°F and grease a 22-cm cake tin.

Prepare the pastry and roll it out. Place it in the prepared tin and chill in the refrigerator while preparing the filling.

To make the filling, beat the egg yolks with the sugar until thick and light. Beat in the cheese, cornflour, vanilla, sour cream and sultanas. Whisk the egg whites until stiff and fold into the cheese mixture. Pour the mixture into the pastry case and bake for about 45 minutes or until golden and firm to the touch. Allow to cool before serving.

SZARLOTKA

APPLE CAKE

1.5 kg apples, peeled, cored and sliced
2 tablespoons sugar
60 g butter
60 g sugar
3 egg yolks
250 g plain flour
1 teaspoon bicarbonate of soda
¼ cup cream
1 teaspoon vanilla essence

Serves 6–8

Preheat the oven to 220°C/425°F and grease a 22-cm cake tin.

Place the apples in a baking tin, sprinkle with the 2 tablespoons of sugar and bake until soft. Cream the butter and 60 g sugar until light and fluffy and add the egg yolks one at a time while still beating. Sift the flour and bicarbonate of soda and fold into the butter mixture together with the cream and vanilla. Divide the mixture into two.

On a lightly floured surface roll each portion of the mixture out until it is the same size as the base of the greased cake tin. Place one portion in the bottom of the cake tin, spoon on the cooked apple mixture and top with the other portion of pastry. Sprinkle with a little additional sugar and bake for about 35 minutes. Test the cake with a skewer; when it comes out clean the cake is cooked.

One of the earliest influences on the Portuguese was the invasion of the Moors. They irrigated the land and planted groves of oranges and almonds, still a feature of the countryside today.

In many parts of Portugal the soil is poor and the land suitable for grazing is limited. Meat tends to be tough and therefore needs long, slow cooking. A national speciality is spit-roasted sucking-pig; the pigs feed on acorns and white truffles and their flesh is sweet and full of flavour.

If meat is generally of poor quality, it is more than compensated for by what the sea has to offer. Portugal is a paradise for lovers of seafood. Fresh mackerel, red mullet, bream, fleshy crayfish, crabs and shrimps abound. Fresh sardines are best simply grilled over hot charcoal and served with rock salt and lemon. Another popular fish dish is bacalhau, a highly nutritious dried salt cod. It is said that there is a different recipe for preparing bacalhau for every day of the year.

The Portuguese have a sweet tooth and produce delicious desserts and sweets using eggs, sugar and almonds. One of these, marmelada, is a confectionary of wonderful colour and taste, made of a thick paste prepared from quinces and sugar.

Olive oil is used extensively in Portuguese cooking, being of a stronger and less refined variety than that used in Spain. It is unusual for fruit and vegetables to be imported and so the availability of these is governed by what is in season. Port and Madiera, however, the two famous drinks of Portugal, are in good supply all year round.

CALDO VERDE

Portugal's best known soup takes its name from the dark green couve (cabbage) from which it is made. This long-stemmed cabbage is difficult to obtain outside Portugal, and the dark green outer leaves of a cabbage can be used as a substitute. It is important that the cabbage be finely chopped, and added only minutes before cooking is finished so it does not become limp.

1½ litres chicken stock
1 onion, peeled and chopped
500 g potatoes, peeled and chopped
2 tablespoons cream
salt and freshly ground pepper
350 g couve or green cabbage, finely
   shredded
8 slices chouriço (smoked, spiced
   sausage)

Serves 4

Place the chicken stock, onion and potatoes in a pan and cook gently for about 25 minutes, or until vegetables are tender. Cool slightly and blend or pass through a sieve. Return to the pan, stir in the cream, and season with salt and pepper. Add the couve, heat gently, but do not allow to boil. Serve at once with a couple of slices of chouriço added to each portion.

SARDINHAS

Fresh sardines are now often available in good fishmongers or markets. They make a good light lunch or appertiser. To prepare this dish you will need a metal fish grill and a barbecue.

1 kg fresh sardines
olive oil
rock salt
freshly ground black pepper
1–2 lemons
chopped parsley

Serves 4

Clean the sardines of their guts and run under a cold tap. Brush a metal fish grill with olive oil and arrange the sardines on it. Cook over a fierce fire, turning to cook both sides. Serve with rock salt, freshly ground black pepper, wedges of lemon and freshly chopped parsley.

LIMÕES RECHEADOS COM SARDINHAS

This recipe is equally good made with canned tuna fish.

6 lemons of uniform size
1 can sardines (100 g)
125 g softened butter
1 small onion, peeled and grated
freshly ground black pepper
1 egg white, beaten until stiff
6 sprigs parsley or 6 lemon leaves

Serves 6

Cut a slice from the base of the lemons (to enable them to stand upright on a plate). Slice the tops off and remove all the pulp with a spoon. Discard all the seeds but reserve the pulp and juice. Mash the sardines until smooth, add the softened butter and onion and season with salt and pepper. Mix well. Add the juice and pulp from the lemons and fold in the egg white. Taste and adjust the seasoning if necessary. Stuff the lemon cases with this mixture and garnish with parsley or lemon leaves.

MIOLOS FRITOS

BRAINS FRIED IN BATTER

1 set brains per person
1 bay leaf
1 small onion
1 sprig parsley
1 small carrot
few drops vinegar
molho de tomate (see below)
massa vinhe (see below)
salt and freshly ground pepper
plain flour
olive oil
1–2 lemons
chopped parsley

Molho de Tomate   (Tomato Sauce)
1 tablespoon butter
6 tablespoons olive oil
1 onion, peeled and chopped
1 carrot, scraped and chopped
1 clove garlic, peeled and crushed
1 kg tomatoes, peeled and chopped
1 teaspoon sugar
pinch of dried thyme or sprig fresh
    thyme
salt and freshly ground black pepper
1 dessertspoon plain flour
1 cup water

Massa Vinhe   (Batter)
225 g plain flour
pinch of salt
3 tablespoons olive oil
3 tablespoons beer
water
2 egg yolks
3 egg whites

Serves 6

Note that the batter for this dish should be made $\frac{1}{2}$ an hour before it is required.

It is most important when preparing brains that they are first left to soak in cold water for $\frac{1}{2}$ an hour. Change the water once during this time. Remove any membranes and then put the brains into a pan with the bay leaf, onion, parsley sprig, carrot and vinegar. Cover with cold water, bring to the boil and simmer gently for 10 minutes. Drain and allow to cool.

To make the tomato sauce, heat the butter and oil in a pan and add the onion, carrot and garlic. Cook over a gentle heat for 5 minutes. Add the tomatoes, sugar and thyme and season with salt and pepper. Simmer gently for 10 minutes. Mix the flour to a thin paste with a little of the water. Add this, with the remaining water, to the pan and stir until the sauce thickens. Pour into a blender and blend until smooth.

To make the massa vinhe, sieve the flour and salt into a bowl. Make a well in the centre and add the oil, beer and a little water. Mix until smooth. Add the egg yolks and stir until blended. Cover and leave for $\frac{1}{2}$ an hour.

Finally, whisk the egg whites until stiff, fold into the batter and use at once. Dust the brains lightly with seasoned flour, dip them in the batter and fry in hot olive oil. Serve with lemon wedges, chopped parsley and the molho de tomate.

FAVAS À RIBATEJANA

BROAD BEANS WITH HAM AND SAUSAGE

250 g belly of pork, chopped
1 onion, peeled and chopped
2 cloves garlic, peeled and crushed
1 kg broad beans
200 g ham, cut into strips
250 g chouriço (smoked spicy sausage),
    sliced
salt and freshly ground black pepper
1 tablespoon chopped parsley

Serves 4–6

Fry the belly of pork in a pan with a heavy base. When the fat has started to run add the onion and the garlic. Fry for about 15 minutes or until pork is cooked.

Fill an enamel saucepan with salted water and when boiling add the beans (a tin pan will turn them black). Cook until tender—about 15–20 minutes. Drain and add to the pork, together with the ham and sausage. Cook over a gentle heat for another 10 minutes, adjust seasoning, garnish with parsley and serve.

BACALHAU DOURADO

European fishermen have been salting and drying cod for centuries. Its yellowish, board-like appearance is somewhat less than attractive, but it is very nutritious. Preparation of the dish needs to start 24 hours before it is to be eaten. The dried salt cod is readily available at most delicatessens.

1 kg bacalhau
2 tablespoons plain flour
olive oil for frying
2 onions, peeled and chopped
400 g canned tomatoes
2 red peppers, seeded and cut
    into strips
2 tablespoons chopped parsley
2 cloves garlic, peeled and crushed
1 glass white wine
salt and freshly ground pepper
1 hardboiled egg, peeled and mashed

Serves 4

Soak the fish in cold water for 24 hours, changing the water two or three times during this period. Place the fish in a large pan, cover with cold water and bring to the boil. Drain and discard the water. Repeat this process once. When the fish has cooled, remove the skin and bones and cut into pieces. Dust lightly with flour, fry in the hot olive oil and drain on kitchen paper. Place in an ovenproof casserole.

Fry the onions in the remaining oil in the pan until soft, but not browned. Add the tomatoes, red peppers, parsley, garlic and white wine. Season with salt and pepper, and simmer for 10 minutes. Pour over the fish in the casserole and bake in a moderate oven at 190°C/375°F for 40 minutes. Garnish with the hardboiled egg and serve.

PUDIM DE NOZES

6 egg yolks
250 g castor sugar
250 g walnuts, crushed between 2 layers
    of waxed paper
1 teaspoon cinnamon
½ teaspoon nutmeg
3 egg whites
butter
whipped cream

Serves 4–6

Beat the egg yolks and sugar until light and fluffy. Add the crushed nuts and spices and mix well. Whisk the egg whites until stiff and carefully fold into the mixture. Generously butter a steamer and pour in the mixture, leaving space at the top for the pudding to expand. Cover with a double layer of waxed paper, and put into a saucepan of water to steam for an hour. Keep checking the water from time to time and if necessary top up with more water. The pudding is set when it is firm to the touch. Turn out of the mould and leave to get cold. Serve with whipped cream.

TARTE DE AMÊNDOA

6 eggs
225 g sugar
140 g plain flour
225 g ground almonds
1 tablespoon brandy

Meringue
3 egg whites
140 g castor sugar
few drops of vinegar

Serves 6

Preheat the oven to 190°C/375°F and generously butter a 28-cm flan tin.

Beat the eggs and sugar until light. Fold in the flour, ground almonds and brandy. Mix well and spoon into the prepared flan tin. Bake in a moderate oven for 30 minutes, or until firm to the touch. Allow to cool.

To prepare the meringue, whisk the egg whites until stiff with a couple of drops of vinegar. Fold in the sugar, a little at a time. Smooth the meringue over the tart and return the tin to a hot oven, 220°C/425°F, and bake until the meringue has browned slightly.

It is scarcely possible to speak of a national cuisine in a country that covers more than one sixth of the earth's land surface, spans several climatic zones and which is inhabited by peoples of many different races and cultures.

Before the 1917 revolution, the diet of the peasants consisted of such basics as black bread and cabbage soup. The aristocracy, in contrast, employed foreign chefs to prepare elaborate meals influenced by the culinary traditions of other lands, particularly France.

For most Russians today, the food they eat is certainly much simpler than that served at the aristocratic banquets of the past. Most women work outside the home so time available for the preparation of food is limited, and the necessity to queue for many items undoubtedly dampens any enthusiasm for experimental cooking. Furthermore, during the harsh winter months fresh fruit and vegetables are difficult to obtain.

The Russian palate favours sour tastes. Bread is made from sour dough; sour cream or smetána is used extensively in cooking; and prostokvasha, a thick sour milk, consumed as it is or made into cheese, is very popular.

Caviar is probably the best-known Russian delicacy, due in part to the large quantities that are exported. Also familiar is shashlik or kebabs, said to have originated in the Caucasus where the warriors threaded meat onto their swords and grilled it over an open fire.

Many items used in Russian cooking such as buckwheat, salted herrings and salted cucumbers, sour cream and yeast are readily available at stores specialising in foreign food.

BÓRSCHT

125 g butter
2 large beetroot, peeled and diced
3 carrots, scraped and diced
1 large onion, peeled and chopped
2 tomatoes, peeled and chopped
2 large potatoes, peeled and diced
2 tablespoons wine vinegar
1 tablespoon sugar
2 litres beef stock
salt and freshly ground black pepper
4 cloves garlic, peeled and crushed
$\frac{3}{4}$ cup sour cream

Serves 6–8

Melt the butter in a large heavy pan, add the beetroot and carrot and cook over a gentle heat for 5 minutes. Add the onion, tomatoes, potatoes, vinegar, sugar and a cup of the stock. Cover and cook over a gentle heat for 30 minutes. Add the remainder of the stock, season with salt and pepper and add the crushed garlic and a little more vinegar if necessary. Cook for another 20 minutes. Turn off the heat and allow to stand for 20 minutes.

You may sieve the soup, which will be a magnificent purple colour, or you may serve it with the vegetables intact. Either way, add a spoon of sour cream before serving. Bórscht can be eaten either hot or cold.

IKRÁ

The preparation of caviar, the roe of the sturgeon, is a complex process, making it an expensive luxury to most people. The best caviar, and the most expensive, is considered to be that obtained from the beluga, the largest member of the sturgeon family. Red caviar is produced from salmon roe and is not as expensive as the black variety.

Serving Suggestions
500 g caviar
1–2 onions
1–2 hardboiled eggs
1 lemon
pure cream or sour cream
brown bread, sliced

Caviar makes an excellent *hors-d'oeuvre*. Serve it in a small bowl set in crushed ice. Finely chop the onion, mash the egg, cut the lemon into thin slices and serve each separately in individual dishes. Place the cream in a bowl. The bread can be spread with caviar and the other accompaniments according to individual taste.

BLINÍ

Bliní are yeast pancakes. They can be made from different types of flour: wheat, buckwheat or rye, or a combination if wished. Allow plenty of time to prepare the bliní as the batter must be allowed to rise twice before cooking.

$3\frac{3}{4}$ cups milk
15 g yeast
500 g plain flour

Heat $\frac{3}{4}$ cup of the milk but do not allow it to boil. Add the yeast and stir until dissolved. Fold in half the flour and mix well. Cover with a cloth and leave to stand in a warm place for about $2\frac{1}{2}$ hours. When it has risen add the beaten egg, melted butter, salt and sugar. Fold in the remaining flour and stir thoroughly. Heat the remainder of the milk, pour it into the batter, stirring to take care it does not become lumpy. Once again cover with a cloth and leave to rest for another 2 hours in a warm place.

Heat a small heavy pan and smear with a film of oil. Using a small jug pour in just enough batter to cover the surface. When small bubbles

1 egg, beaten
3 tablespoons melted butter
1 teaspoon salt
1 tablespoon sugar
oil

Serving Suggestions
sour cream
smoked salmon
salted fish, sliced
caviar
onion, finely chopped
melted buter

Serves 6–8

appear it is ready to turn. It may take a little practice to perfect this procedure as the heat of the pan and the amount of oil can affect the end result. When the bliní are cooked on both sides, stack in a buttered bowl. They can be covered and used later. Serve them piled on a plate accompanied by sour cream, smoked salmon, salted sliced fish, caviar, finely chopped onion or melted butter.

KÁSHA

CHEESE AND BUCKWHEAT PATTIES

Kásha is made from buckwheat. It can be served in various ways: as an accompaniment to soups and meat dishes, or it can be made into puddings.

½ teaspoon salt
2 cups of water
250 g buckwheat
125 g cream cheese
2 eggs, beaten
1½ teaspoons sugar
1 cup fresh white breadcrumbs
butter or oil for frying
sour cream for garnishing

Makes about 12 patties

Bring the salted water to the boil in a large pan. Sprinkle in the buckwheat and cook for about ½ an hour. Allow to stand until it has thickened and then put through a blender or push through a fine sieve. Add the cream cheese, eggs and sugar and mix well. Form the mixture into flat patties, roll in the breadcrumbs and fry in hot butter or oil until golden. Serve with sour cream.

PELMÉNY

MEAT DUMPLINGS FROM SIBERIA

250 g plain flour
1 egg
salt
2–3 tablespoons cold water
375 g lean pork
1 onion, peeled
pepper
boiling water or stock
sour cream

Makes about 12–14 dumplings

Sift the flour into a bowl, make a well in the centre and break the egg into it. Add a good pinch of salt and start mixing, adding the cold water at the same time. Mix until you have a firm dough. Leave covered in a cool place for about 30 minutes.

Mince together the pork and the onion, season with salt and pepper and moisten with a little water.

On a floured board roll out the dough until very thin. Cut out circles about 5 cm in diameter. Put a little of the meat filling on one half of the round, fold over and pinch the edges together to secure. Continue this procedure until all the mixture has been used up. Cook in a large pan of boiling water, or if preferred, use stock. The dumplings will rise to the surface when cooked. Serve with melted butter, sour cream or in a bowl of broth.

BYEF-STRÓGANOV

This dish is said to have been invented by Count Stroganoff's chef, who discovered that his meat had become frozen and could only be cut into very fine strips. Although the dish is widely known in the West, it is rarely served in Russian homes today. One will find it, however, served in restaurants catering for the tourist trade.

90 g butter
1 onion, peeled and chopped
750 g fillet or rump steak, cut into thin
    strips
125 g mushrooms, wiped with a damp
    cloth and sliced
salt and freshly ground black pepper
1 dessertspoon plain flour
pinch of mustard
1¼ cups sour cream

Serves 4

Melt the butter in a large pan and sauté the onion until golden. Add the sliced meat and cook until lightly browned. Add the mushrooms, season with salt and pepper and cook over a gentle heat for 5 minutes.

Mix the flour, mustard and sour cream together, add to the pan and stir to amalgamate all the juices. Simmer gently for 5–10 minutes or until the meat is tender. Add a little more sour cream just befor serving. Mashed potatoes make a good vegetable accompaniment.

KAPUSTNIE OLÁDJI

½ small cabbage
2 cups plain flour
1 egg
2 cups milk
salt and pepper
4 tablespoons butter
1 cup sour cream
grated Parmesan cheese

Serves 4

Chop the cabbage finely and remove the core. Place into a pot of boiling salted water, leave for one minute and then drain.

Sift the flour into a bowl, make a well in the centre, add the egg and gradually pour in the milk, taking care to keep the mixture smooth. Season with the salt and pepper and add the cabbage. Heat a little butter in a frying pan and cook a ladleful of batter at a time, turning to brown on both sides. Keep warm while cooking the rest of the pancakes.

To serve, roll the pancakes, pour some sour cream over them and sprinkle with the Parmesan.

VENIGRET

500 g potatoes, peeled, boiled and diced
1 large carrot, cooked and diced
1 large beetroot, cooked and diced
1 salted cucumber, diced
1 onion, peeled and chopped
125 g pickled cabbage, chopped

Dressing
3 tablespoons oil
1 tablespoon vinegar
1 teaspoon sugar
½ teaspoon mustard
salt and freshly ground pepper

Serves 4

Place all the vegetables in a bowl. Mix the ingredients for the dressing and pour over the salad, tossing to distribute the liquid evenly.

If you wish to make this dish more substantial, chopped hardboiled eggs and pieces of salted herring may be added after it has been dressed.

KULÍCH

This is a traditional Russian cake served at Easter.

500 g plain flour
185 g butter
185 g dark brown sugar
185 g blanched almonds
grated rind of 1 orange
3 eggs, beaten
150 ml milk
1 tablespoon honey
1 tablespoon bicarbonate of soda

Decoration
3 tablespoons sugar
3 tablespoons water
1 oz blanched almonds

Serves 6–8

Grease a 20-cm cake tin with butter and line it with waxed paper. Pre-heat the oven to 160°C/325°F.

Sieve the flour into a large bowl and rub in the butter. Add the sugar, the finely chopped almonds and the grated orange peel. Slowly pour on the beaten eggs with half the milk to bring the mixture to the consistency of a stiff dough.

Dissolve the honey in the rest of the milk and stir in the bicarbonate of soda. When the soda is dissolved add this liquid to the dough, blending together gently to form a mixture which will drop from the spoon. Bake for about 1½ hours.

Make a syrup with the sugar and the water. Just as the syrup starts to colour add the blanched almonds and cook for one minute. Spoon them immediately over the top of the cake where they will set in position.

PÁSKHA

This cake is traditionally served during the Russian Easter as an accompaniment to Kulich. It would have the place of honour on the table, surrounded by brightly coloured and decorated hardboiled eggs. Its traditional shape is vertical and a plastic flower pot is a good substitute if no other vertical mould is available.

250 g seedless raisins
500 g cream cheese
¾ cup sour cream
125 g butter
250 g castor sugar
½ teaspoon vanilla
½ teaspoon almond essence
125 g candied peel, chopped
125 g blanched almonds
pinch of salt

Serves 6

Soak the raisins in hot water until they are plump and then drain. Blend the cream cheese, sour cream, butter and sugar until smooth. Add all the other ingredients and stir thoroughly. The mixture should be firm. Using some clean muslin line a mould with a perforated base. Spoon the mixture into this, place a weight on top and allow to stand in a cool place for 12 hours. Turn out and serve.

Denmark, Sweden, Finland, Iceland and Norway together comprise the region known as Scandinavia. Although there are significant differences between each country, the food does display many similarities. Generally speaking, the fisherman and the hunter are relatively more important than is the case in the rest of Europe. Fish is a particularly important source of food and it appears in most meals in some form.

The cuisine of Denmark is more European than that of the other Scandinavian countries. The smørrebrød or Danish open sandwich is Denmark's own speciality, however, famous throughout the world. Thin slices of buttered rye or crisp bread are covered with an artisitically arranged assortment of toppings, usually including something smoked, spiced or pickled to add a sharp taste. The combinations are virtually limitless.

The Danish attitude toward alcohol differs from that of other Scandinavian countries and both beer and schnapps are available at all hours.

The smörgåsbord is to Sweden what the smørrebrød is to Denmark. It consists typically of five courses. The first is fish such as herrings (sometimes pickled), salmon, eels or sardines. A hot dish is always included, possibly some form of beef or smoked reindeer meat. Salads, eggs and cheese follow and the meal concludes with fruit and more cheese. Most courses in a smörgåsbord can also be served as individual supper dishes.

The potato is the staple of Finnish agriculture while the lakes and forests provide good fish and game. Excellent fruit soups provide refreshment for the most jaded palate. Sweden, Finland and Norway have strict laws governing the consumption of alcohol and Finns often drink buttermilk with their meals.

The Norwegian version of the smörgåsbord is the kolde bord. Again, fish predominates, especially cod. Pork is the most popular meat but roasted venison is also prepared, accompanied by a special sauce made from goat's cheese and redcurrant jelly.

SCANDINAVIA: Smørrebrød (Danish Open Sandwiches). See page 98.

GULE AERTER (DENMARK)
ÄRTER MED FLÄSK (SWEDEN)

YELLOW PEA SOUP

This recipe has many variations. Smoked pork, bacon or sausage can be added, depending on your taste.

300 g yellow split peas (soaked in cold water for at least 2 hours)
2½ litres water
salt and freshly ground black pepper
500 g piece smoked bacon
bouquet of herbs (1 bay leaf, 2 sprigs each of parsley, thyme, marjoram)
6 onions, peeled and chopped
4 sticks celery, chopped
250 g carrots, peeled and chopped
3 leeks, carefully washed and sliced
500 g potatoes, peeled and diced
½ teaspoon powdered ginger
4 smoked frankfurters

Serves 8

Cook the peas in 1 litre of the water over a low heat until tender (about 1½–2 hours). Blend until smooth and season with salt and pepper.

Put the piece of bacon in a pan with the remaining water and herbs, cover and simmer for an hour. Add the vegetables and ginger and simmer for a further hour. Remove the bacon and cut into bite-sized pieces.

Stir the pea purée into the pan with the vegetables, adjust the seasoning and add more water if the soup is too thick. Reheat the soup, adding the frankfurters and bacon 5 minutes before serving. Place in large bowls, with rye bread as an accompaniment.

LEVERPOSTEJ

LIVER PÂTÉ (DENMARK AND SWEDEN)

1 pigs liver (about 750 g)
2 onions, peeled
155 g lard
4 anchovy fillets or 1 dessertspoon anchovy essence
salt and freshly ground black pepper
1 tablespoon sugar
sprig fresh marjoram or ½ teaspoon dried marjoram
2 eggs
125 g plain flour
2½ cups milk
100 g butter, melted

Serves 8–10

Preheat the oven to 180°C/350°F.

Put the liver, onions, lard and anchovy fillets through a mincer twice. Season generously with the salt, pepper and sugar. Add the marjoram and mix well.

Whisk the eggs in a bowl, sift in the flour and add the milk, stirring to a smooth paste. Add this to the minced liver, along with the melted butter.

Butter a pâté dish or ovenproof casserole (with a lid), add the pâté mixture, cover with a double layer of greaseproof paper and place the lid on top. Stand in a pan of water and bake in a moderate oven for about an hour. The pâté will shrink away from the sides slightly when cooked. It will have a rough texture and if a smoother pâté is preferred, blend the ingredients instead of putting them through a mincer. Serve as part of a smörgåsbord, or sliced, with buttered toast as an accompaniment.

ROCQUEFORD DRESSING

DANISH BLUE DRESSING

¾ cup salad oil
⅓ cup lemon juice
1 teaspoon salt
1 teaspoon paprika
1 teaspoon sugar
125 g Danish blue cheese, mashed into fine crumbs

Mix all the ingredients in a pestle and mortar until smooth. Serve with salads.

RUSSIA: Bórscht. See page 92.

SMØRREBRØD

OPEN SANDWICHES (DENMARK)

Suggested Toppings

**smoked salmon with sour cream and
  caviar**
**smoked eel with scrambled egg and
  raw onion**
**rare roast beef with horseradish and
  watercress**
**prawns with hardboiled egg, cucumber
  and mayonnaise**
**ham or chicken fillets with cucumber
  and redcurrant jelly**
**'Union Jack' (finely minced raw fillet
  steak, onion ring, egg yolk, shrimps)**

These Danish open sandwiches have as their base a thin slice of buttered rye or crisp bread. As mentioned in the introduction, the topping combinations are countless.

The 'Union Jack' is a famous topping, first made to celebrate Denmark's liberation in 1945. Place the finely minced raw fillet steak on the buttered bread, hollow out the centre and lie the onion ring in the space. Inside this drop the egg yolk. Place a circle of small pink shrimps around the edge of the onion ring.

AEBLEKAGE

DANISH APPLE CAKE

125 g butter
125 g castor sugar
125 g plain flour
1 egg
500 g cooking apples, peeled and sliced
2 tablespoons sultanas
1 teaspoon cinnamon
1 teaspoon ginger
1 dessertspoon lemon juice
1 tablespoon brown sugar
2 tablespoons chopped walnuts

Preheat the oven to 180°C/350°F and grease a 22-cm cake tin.

Melt the butter and mix with the sugar. Add the flour gradually and then mix in the egg. Spread two-thirds of the mixture on the bottom of the prepared cake tin, place half the sliced apples on top and sprinkle with the sultanas, cinnamon, ginger, lemon juice and brown sugar. Cover with the remaining apples and sprinkle with the chopped nuts. Place the remaining cake mix on top and bake for 25–30 minutes or until the cake is firm.

SMÅ KÖTTBULLAR

MEAT BALLS (SWEDEN)

This dish is traditionally served with noodles.

3 tablespoons butter
1 onion, peeled and chopped
1 cup mashed potatoes
½ cup fresh breadcrumbs
500 g minced beef
1 egg
⅓ cup cream
2 tablespoons finely chopped parsley
salt and freshly ground pepper
2 tablespoons oil

Sauce
1 tablespoon plain flour
¾ cup cream

Serves 4

Melt 1 tablespoon of the butter and sauté the onion until soft. Place the onion, mashed potatoes, breadcrumbs, minced beef, egg, cream and parsley in a large bowl. Mix well and season with salt and pepper. Form into small balls about 3 cm in diameter. Place on a baking tray and refrigerate for 1 hour before cooking.

Melt the rest of the butter, add the oil and when hot fry the meat balls, turning to brown on all sides. When cooked (about 10 minutes) transfer to a heatproof dish and keep warm. Reserve the pan juices.

To make the sauce, add the flour to the juices in the pan and stir with a wooden spoon to form a smooth paste. Slowly pour in the cream, stirring constantly until the sauce thickens. Pour the sauce over the meat balls and serve with noodles.

KUKT LAMM MED DILL SÅS   BOILED LAMB WITH DILL SAUCE (SWEDEN)

1.5 kg shoulder of lamb
1 bay leaf
6 peppercorns
1 small bunch parsley
1 small bunch dill (additional dill can be used for garnishing)
piece lemon rind
1 onion, peeled and stuck with 3 cloves
1 teaspoon salt
3 carrots, scraped
1–2 lemons for garnishing

Sauce
3 tablespoons butter
3 tablespoons plain flour
1½ cups stock (reserved after cooking the lamb)
2 teaspoons sugar
2 tablespoons white vinegar
2 tablespoons lemon juice
1 small bunch fresh dill, chopped, or 1 teaspoon dried dill
1 egg yolk
3 tablespoons cream

Serves 6–8

Place the meat in a large pot and cover with water. Add the bay leaf, peppercorns, parsley, dill, lemon rind and onion stuck with cloves. Season with the salt, bring to the boil and simmer until the meat is tender (about 2 hours). After about 1½ hours add the carrots. When cooking is completed, remove the meat and carrots and keep warm while preparing the sauce. Strain and reserve the stock.

To make the sauce, melt the butter, spoon in the flour and cook, stirring, for 5 minutes. Slowly add the stock, stirring constantly. Add the sugar, vinegar, lemon juice and dill and simmer until the sauce thickens. In a separate bowl whisk the egg yolk with the cream, mix with 2 tablespoons of the hot stock and add to the sauce. Do not allow the sauce to boil after you have added the egg mixture.

Cut the meat and the carrots into slices and arrange on a serving dish. Pour a little of the sauce over the meat and garnish with slices of fresh lemon and fresh dill. Serve the rest of the sauce separately.

GAASESTEG MED AEBLER OG SVEDSKER   GOOSE STUFFED WITH PRUNES AND APPLES (SWEDEN)

1 goose (about 6 kg)
½ lemon
salt and freshly ground black pepper
6 large apples, peeled and sliced
30 pitted prunes
2 teaspoons caraway seeds

Sauce
2 tablespoons cornflour
2 cups stock (either goose or chicken)

Serves 8–10

Preheat the oven to 160°C/325°F.

Wash the goose and remove any surplus fat from inside the cavity. Rub over with the lemon and sprinkle with a little salt and pepper.

Mix the apples, prunes and caraway seeds and stuff the goose. Skewer or stitch the openings shut. Stand on a rack in a baking tin and cook in a slow oven for 4–4½ hours. Prick the goose with a fork—it is ready when the juices emitted are yellow rather than pink. Remove the goose and keep warm.

To make the sauce, pour off the surplus fat from the pan. Add the cornflour and stir with a wooden spoon until all the bits in the pan have been amalgamated. Add the stock and continue to cook, stirring until the sauce has boiled and thickened. Strain and serve with the goose.

SILLSALLAD

6 pickled herring fillets
2 cold boiled potatoes
1 apple, peeled and cored
1 pickled cucumber
1 small onion, peeled
1 pickled beetroot, chopped
freshly ground black pepper
beetroot juice
hardboiled eggs and sour cream for
  garnish

Serves 4–6

Cut the fish, potatoes, apple, cucumber and onion into cubes. Mix with the beetroot and season with pepper. Pour a little beetroot juice over the salad, cover and refrigerate for several hours. Garnish with hardboiled eggs and serve with a bowl of sour cream.

ÄPPELKAKA

2 kg cooking apples
juice of 1 lemon
sugar
125 g butter
125 g toasted breadcrumbs
125 g castor sugar
cream or custard

Serves 6–8

Preheat the oven to 190°C/375°F.
   Peel, core and slice the apples and cook in a saucepan with the lemon juice and a little water until they form a thick purée. Add sugar to taste.
   In a separate pan melt the butter and fry the breadcrumbs and castor sugar. Grease a shallow cake tin and coat with a layer of the breadcrumbs. Add a layer of the apple mixture, and then a layer of the breadcrumbs. Repeat this procedure until you have three layers, ending with breadcrumbs. Bake in a moderately hot oven for about $\frac{1}{2}$ an hour until the crumbs are browned. Cool for about 10 minutes before turning out onto a serving dish. Serve with cream or custard.

MANDELFYLLDA STEKTA ÄPPLEN

1 cup ground almonds
$\frac{1}{4}$ cup icing sugar
$\frac{1}{4}$ cup water
2 egg whites
6 cooking apples of uniform size
2 tablespoons melted butter
$\frac{1}{2}$ cup dried breadcrumbs

Serves 6

Preheat the oven to 180°C/350°F.
   Place the almonds, sugar, water and unbeaten egg whites into a blender and blend until they form a smooth paste.
   Peel the apples and remove the core, leaving a small portion at the bottom of each apple. Brush the apples with the melted butter and roll in the breadcrumbs. Fill the cavities in the apples with the almond paste and spread any remaining paste on top of the apples. Arrange them just touching in an ovenproof dish. Bake in a moderate oven for about 35 minutes, or until the apples are tender when tested with a skewer.

VANILJSÅS

3 egg yolks
$\frac{1}{4}$ cup castor sugar
1 teaspoon vanilla
$1\frac{1}{2}$ cups cream

Serves 6

It is best to use a double boiler in the preparation of this custard. If not, sit a heatproof bowl in a pan of simmering water. Beat the egg yolks, sugar, vanilla and 1 cup of the cream in the top of the double boiler or bowl. Continue to cook, stirring constantly until the sauce thickens. Do not allow it to boil. Stir the sauce until it cools. Whip the remaining cream and fold it into the cooled sauce. Serve with baked apples or other fruit dessert.

GLÖGG

1 bottle red wine
3 tablespoons schnapps or vodka
½ teaspoon ground ginger
1 cinnamon stick
½ teaspoon cardamom seeds
6 cloves
⅓ cup seedless raisins
⅓ cup blanched almonds

Place the alcohol, ginger, cinnamon stick, cardamom and cloves into a pan and allow to stand for ½ an hour. Put the raisins and almonds in to a large jug. Heat the ingredients in the pan until almost boiling, pour over the raisins and almonds in the jug and serve while still hot.

KIISSELI

This delicious chilled soup is best made when there is a wide variety of fresh fruit available.

4 cups water
1–2 tablespoons sugar
juice of 1 lemon
1.5 kg assorted fruit in season (e.g. nectarines, plums, strawberries, pears, apricots)
½ teaspoon ground cinnamon
½ cup sour cream

Serves 6

Place the water, sugar and lemon juice in a large pan and stir over a gentle heat until the sugar has dissolved. Add the fruit and cinnamon, cover and simmer until the fruit is soft. Pass through a sieve or blend until smooth. Serve chilled with sour cream.

KALA FRIKADELLER

500 g firm white fish fillets
80 g plain flour
salt and freshly ground pepper
1 egg
1¾ cups milk
100 g butter

Makes 8–10 patties

Mince the fish, add the flour and season with salt and pepper. Mix well. Beat the egg in a separate bowl and add to the fish mixture. Slowly add the milk, beating all the time. Do not add more milk until the first lot is completely blended with the fish. The fish mixture must remain quite firm so the actual amount of milk depends on the type of fish used. Melt the butter in a pan. Make the fish into patties and fry, a few at a time, turning to brown both sides. About 5 minutes on each side should be sufficient. Do not let the pan get too hot. Drain on absorbent paper.

KARJALANPAISTI

250 g pork
250 g beef
250 g lamb
125 g kidneys
125 g calves liver
1 onion, peeled and sliced
2 bay leaves
6 whole allspice
salt and freshly ground pepper

Serves 4–6

Cut the meat into bite-sized pieces and place it in an earthenware casserole. Cover with the sliced onion, add the bay leaves and allspice and season with salt and pepper. Pour enough cold water into the casserole to cover the meat and cook in a slow oven at 150°C/300°F for about 4 hours.

POTATISKAKA MED OST-KASEROSTI

POTATO CAKE
WITH CHEESE (FINLAND)

750 g potatoes
2 large onions
4 tablespoons butter
155 g Gruyère cheese, grated
salt

Serves 4

Peel and grate the potatoes and onions coarsely. Melt the butter in a large frying pan and cook the potatoes and onions gently for about 10 minutes. Add 60 g of the grated cheese and stir to mix. Flatten the mixture with an egg slice and fry gently until crisp and golden on the bottom. Carefully turn the cake over and brown on the other side. Sprinkle with the rest of the cheese and allow to melt. Serve at once.

PORKKANA VANUKAS

CARROT PUDDING (FINLAND)

½ cup pearl barley
2 cups water
2 cups boiling milk
500 g carrots, scraped and grated
1 beaten egg
2 teaspoons sugar
salt
breadcumbs
butter

Serves 4

Put the barley into a medium-sized pan, add the water and cook over a moderate heat. Gradually add the boiling milk and cook for an hour. Add the grated carrots, egg and sugar and season with salt. Mix well and pour the mixture into a buttered ovenproof dish, sprinkle with fresh breadcrumbs and dot with butter. Bake in a moderate oven for 1 hour.

SOLÖYE

SUN'S EYE OR POLAR BEAR'S EYE (NORWAY)

60 g parsley, finely chopped
10 anchovies, chopped
1 potato, boiled and finely chopped
4 tablespoons raw onion, finely
    chopped
1 cooked beetroot, peeled and finely
    chopped
4 egg yolks, beaten
rye bread and butter for serving

Serves 4

Choose four serving plates, preferably plain and white. Make a circle on the plates with the parsley, anchovies, potato, onion and beetroot. Carefully pour a raw egg yolk into the middle of the circle on each plate and serve with rye bread and butter.

BIRGITTE SALAT

250 g cooked white fish
1 orange
125 g cooked peas
125 g grated raw carrots
1 apple, peeled and grated
2 gherkins chopped
1 lettuce

Dressing
2 tablespoons wine vinegar
2 tablespoons oil
3 tablespoons water
2 tablespoons sugar
$\frac{1}{2}$ teaspoon salt
$\frac{1}{2}$ teaspoon paprika

Serves 4

Remove the bones from the fish and divide the flesh into bite-sized pieces. Peel the orange, remove the pith, and cut the flesh into pieces. Carefully mix the fish and vegetables in a bowl. Mix all other ingredients into a dressing, and pour over the salad. This dish can be served on lettuce leaves.

JANSSONS FRESTELSE

125 g butter
2 onions, peeled and sliced
5 medium potatoes, peeled and thinly
    sliced
freshly ground black pepper
1 small can anchovies
1 cup cream

Serves 4

Melt enough butter in a pan to sauté the onions until soft. Butter a casserole and place half the potatoes in it. Season with a little pepper, spread the onions on top, then the anchovies and finish with the rest of the potatoes. Dot the remainder of the butter over the potatoes and place in a moderate oven for 10 minutes. Remove the dish and pour in half the cream. Replace the casserole in the oven and cook for another 10 minutes. Add the remainder of the cream and continue cooking until the potatoes are done—about 1 hour. Serve with a green salad.

HIMMELSK LAPSKAUS

1 large banana, peeled and chopped
1 cup seeded grapes, cut in halves
$\frac{1}{2}$ cup chopped walnuts, pecans or
    almonds
1 cup chopped apples or oranges

Sauce
5 egg yolks
2 egg whites
75 g castor sugar
1 tablespoon brandy

Serves 4–6

Place the fruit and nuts into a serving dish, toss to mix and chill while preparing the sauce. In a separate bowl whip the egg yolks, whites and sugar together until thick and creamy. Fold in the brandy. Serve the sauce with the fruit.

When the Romans conquered Spain, they brought with them the olive tree which provided the foundation of modern Spanish cuisine. The influence of the Moors remains important, too, and is reflected in the use made of citrus fruit, rice, saffron, and nuts, all of which they introduced.

Most of the world's finest green olives are grown around Seville. Olives are not only eaten as tapas (snacks) to be consumed with drinks but are used in many dishes. Spanish olive oil is thought by some to be heavy, but this is not the case if it is made sufficiently hot before cooking commences. Spaniards also often fry a piece of bread in the oil to eliminate some of the grease.

Two large meals are eaten each day, breakfast consisting only of coffee and bread. Lunch is served around 2 p.m. and might comprise soup, a fish or meat dish, salad or vegetables and perhaps some cheese. Desserts are rare. The meal is washed down with copious quantities of Spanish wine and needless to say, a siesta follows. Work resumes around 4 p.m. and the evening meal, similar in content to lunch, is eaten no earlier than 9 p.m. and sometimes after midnight.

The Spanish keep their hunger at bay by nibbling on tapas all day; these might include little canapés and small dishes. Tapas translates as either 'blotting paper' or, according to some, 'lid', which refers to an old Spanish custom of covering one's glass with a slice of bread in order to keep the flies out.

Food is prepared in a fairly relaxed manner in Spain; no special skills are required, although an ability to improvise helps and dishes tend to vary according to what is immediately to hand. Cooking is not confined to the kitchen and it is not unusual to see a paella (a delicious rice dish) being cooked on the beach over an open fire.

GAZPACHO

ICED CUCUMBER, GREEN PEPPER AND TOMATO SOUP

1 kg tomatoes
boiling water
1 green pepper, seeded and finely
  chopped
1 thick slice stale brown bread
1 small onion, peeled and chopped
3 cloves garlic, peeled and crushed
½ cucumber, peeled and diced
1½ cups chicken stock or water
2 tablespoons olive oil
1 tablespoon vinegar
salt and freshly ground black pepper
1 tablespoon sugar
juice of ½ lemon
ice cubes

Serves 4–8

Spain's most famous soup is both refreshing and delicious. All the ingredients are fresh and no cooking is required. Gazpacho can be made in a blender, but it is best when chopped by hand. If packed in a thermos, gazpacho makes excellent picnic food.

Plunge the tomatoes into boiling water for 2 minutes (this loosens the skins), peel and seed them and chop the flesh to a pulp. Add the green pepper to the tomatoes.

Trim the crusts from the bread and discard. Cut the bread into cubes. Add the onion, garlic, bread and cucumber to the tomato mixture. Add the stock, olive oil, vinegar, salt, pepper, sugar and lemon juice to taste. Chill in the refrigerator for several hours and serve with cubes of ice floating in the soup.

SOPA DE AJO AL HUEVO

SOUP WITH GARLIC AND EGG

Sopa de ajo, or garlic soup, is one of Spain's most popular dishes. Spaniards add a variety of ingredients to it—eggs (as shown here), almonds or bread for example.

5 tablespoons olive oil
3 cloves garlic, peeled
4 thick slices bread
5 cups chicken stock
1 teaspoon paprika
salt and freshly ground black pepper
2 eggs, lightly beaten

Serves 4

Preheat the oven to 230°C/450°F.

Heat the oil in a large pan and fry the garlic cloves until lightly browned. Remove the garlic. Trim the crusts from the bread and discard. Fry the bread on both sides. Bring the chicken stock to boiling point and ladle it over the bread in the pan, add the paprika and season with salt and pepper. Cover and simmer for 10 minutes.

Spoon the beaten eggs over the top of the soup to form a layer on the surface. Place in the oven and cook until a golden crust forms on the surface. Serve at once.

TORTILLA ESPAÑOLA

SPANISH OMELETTE

¼ cup olive oil
1 medium onion, peeled and sliced
3 medium potatoes, peeled and sliced
salt and freshly ground black pepper
8 eggs
2 tablespoons cold water

Serves 4

This heavy omelette is one of Spain's most popular dishes. Ingredients can vary according to what you have in the cupboard.

Heat the oil in a large omelette pan and cook the onion until it begins to soften. Add the sliced potatoes and fry until golden. Season with salt and black pepper.

Beat the eggs in a bowl and add the water while still beating. Pour the eggs over the potato and onion mixture and allow to cook. Quickly turn and brown the other side and serve at once.

PIMIENTOS RELLENOS ESTILO AVILES   STUFFED GREEN PEPPERS

Peppers were first brought to Spain by Spanish explorers returning from Mexico but originally were used only for decorative purposes.

½ cup olive oil
8 large green peppers
1 large onion, peeled and chopped
3 cloves garlic, peeled and crushed
3 large tomatoes, peeled, seeded and
    chopped
½ cup white wine
salt and freshly ground black pepper
1 teaspoon sugar
1 cup cooked rice
250 g ham, chopped

Serves 4 6

Preheat the oven to 180°C/350°F.

Pour a little of the oil into a baking dish, roll the peppers in it to coat them and bake for 10 minutes. Remove from the oven and allow to cool slightly. Cut the tops from the peppers and reserve. Remove the seeds and core and discard.

Heat the remaining oil in a medium-sized pan and sauté the onion and garlic until golden. Add the tomatoes and wine, season with salt, pepper and sugar and simmer for 10 minutes. Add the cooked rice and chopped ham and mix well. Stuff the peppers with this mixture, return their tops, place upright in a baking dish and cook in the preheated oven for about 20 minutes, or until the peppers are tender. Serve hot or cold.

PIPERADE   SPANISH RATATOUILLE

1 kg red and green peppers
¾ cup olive oil
3 onions, peeled and chopped
3 cloves garlic, peeled and crushed
1.5 kg tomatoes, peeled
sprig fresh thyme or ½ teaspoon dried
    thyme
salt and freshly ground black pepper
6 slices Basque ham or Italian
    prosciutto
1 egg per person (optional)

Serves 6

This dish comes from the Basque region of Spain—on the northern border with south-west France.

Seed and core the peppers and cut into strips. Heat the oil in a large pan and cook the onions. Add the garlic and peppers and cook until soft. Chop the tomatoes and add with the thyme to the peppers and onions. Season to taste with salt and pepper. Fry the ham in a separate pan, then add to the sauce. Simmer for 5 minutes. If desired, the piperade can be served with fried eggs.

CALAMARES FRITOS   FRIED SQUID

olive oil for frying
500 g squid, cleaned and cut into rings
    (the fishmonger will usually do this)
185 g plain flour
3 eggs, beaten
salt and freshly ground black pepper
wedges of lemon

Serves 4

Heat the olive oil in a medium-sized pan until smoking. Dip the squid into the flour. Season the beaten eggs with salt and pepper and then dip the squid into this mixture. Fry until golden (do not overcook or the squid will become tough). Drain on kitchen paper and serve at once, accompanied by the lemon.

PAELLA

SAFFRON RICE WITH POULTRY, SEAFOOD AND VEGETABLES

1 medium chicken (fresh not frozen,
  if possible)
3 tablespoons olive oil
1 onion, peeled and chopped
2 cloves garlic, peeled and crushed
250 g long grain rice
boiling water
salt and freshly ground black pepper
1 bay leaf
½ teaspoon powdered saffron
12 mussels, thoroughly cleaned
16 large prawns
500 g peas, shelled
1 red pepper, seeded and chopped
2 tomatoes, peeled and chopped
6 artichoke hearts, quartered
1 small cooked lobster (optional)

Serves 6

Paella is probably Spain's best known dish. Its name comes from the heavy oval pan with two handles in which the meal is cooked and usually served. Paellas vary enormously, and it is often said no two are ever the same. However, the dish always has saffron flavoured rice as its base with additions of poultry, shellfish and vegetables.

Roast the chicken, allow to cool slightly, then cut into about 12 pieces. Heat 2 tablespoons of the oil in a large pan and sauté the onion and garlic. When the onion is just tender, add the rice and cook while stirring for a couple of minutes. Cover with boiling water. Season, add the bay leaf and the saffron. Cook on a high heat for about 15 minutes (the cooking time will depend on the type of rice used), stirring frequently and adding more water if necessary. Meanwhile steam the cleaned mussels until they open and shell the prawns, leaving about four with their heads and tails intact for garnishing. If lobster is being used, cut it into bite-sized pieces.

Cook the peas and fry the pepper and tomatoes in the remaining oil. Just before the rice is cooked, stir in all the other ingredients and adjust the seasoning. Serve as soon as the rice is ready, preferably in the pan in which it was cooked. Garnish with the whole prawns.

TORRIJAS

CRISP BREAD FINGERS IN A LEMON SYRUP

8 slices day-old white bread
1 cup milk
1 egg, beaten
oil for frying

Syrup
125 g sugar
150 ml water
piece lemon rind
½ teaspoon ground cinnamon
150 ml sherry

Serves 4

Make the syrup first. Place the sugar and water in a pan over a gentle heat and stir until the sugar has dissolved. Add the lemon rind and cinnamon and continue to cook until a syrup forms (about 10 minutes). Allow to cool and add the sherry.

Trim the crusts from the bread and discard. Cut the bread into fingers and first soak them in the milk, and then in the beaten egg. Heat the oil in a small pan and fry the fingers, a few at a time, until golden. Place them in a mound on a serving dish and pour the cool syrup over the top. Serve at once.

SANGRIA

RED WINE PUNCH

3 limes or 2 lemons
1 bottle good red wine (preferably
  claret)
1 bottle lemonade, chilled
1 generous wineglass brandy
ice cubes (optional)
sliced orange or lime for serving
fresh mint for serving

Serves 6–8

Squeeze the limes or lemons and strain the juice. Put all the ingredients into a large jug. Ice can be added to keep the sangria icy cold but remember that as it melts it will dilute the punch. If desired, a sliced orange or lime and a little fresh mint can be added for serving.

Switzerland has been strongly influenced by neighbouring Germany, Italy and France and this is reflected in regional differences in food. Among the German-speaking Swiss of the north, sausages and beer are popular, while in the south the flavour of Italy predominates in macaroni, minestrone, polenta, ravioli and risotto.

French is the language of the west and much of the food from this region has cheese as an ingredient. Switzerland is famous for its dairy produce and the renowned Gruyère and Emmenthal cheeses come from this area. A local speciality is a cheese soup, made by adding an egg to grated cheese and pouring a boiling broth containing potatoes and onions over the top.

Fondue is eaten as a communal dish from a caquelon *(a special cooking pot for fondue) placed over a small spirit stove. The diners are supplied with long-handled forks which they use to spear pieces of bread, meat, fruit, etc. and dip them into the fondue which can consist of cheese, oil or chocolate. Freshwater fish, served in the summer months, is another Swiss speciality.*

MUESLI

2 level tablespoons rolled oats
6 tablespoons water
2 tablespoons cream
1 teaspoon honey
juice of 1 lemon
2 fruits of your choice
1 tablespoon nuts (hazelnuts, almonds,
walnuts, etc.), chopped

Serves 1

Muesli was invented by Dr Bircher-Benner, a pioneer of food reform, for patients at his Zürich clinic. While peaches, apples, nectarines, apricots and bananas suit muesli especially well, any fruit can be used. You will need to start preparing the muesli the night before it is required.

Place the rolled oats in a bowl with the water and allow to soak overnight. Next morning, stir in the cream, honey and lemon juice. Peel the fruit if desired, slice it thinly and add to the muesli. If using apple, grate it unpeeled. Add the nuts and serve.

OEUFS À LA SUISSE

butter
6 tablespoons grated Gruyère or
Emmenthal cheese
4 tablespoons cream
4 eggs
salt and freshly ground black pepper
extra cream

Serves 4

Preheat the oven to 190°C/375°F.

Butter four small ovenproof dishes (about 9 cm in diameter) and cover the bottom of each with a thick layer of grated cheese. Add a tablespoon of cream to each dish and make a slight cavity in the cheese. Carefully break an egg on to the cream. Dust each egg lightly with salt and pepper, spoon a little more cream over the eggs and sprinkle with more grated cheese. Cook in a moderately hot oven for 10–15 minutes and serve at once.

FONDUE AU FROMAGE

1 clove garlic, peeled and halved
2½ cups dry white wine
750 g Gruyère cheese, grated
2 teaspoons cornflour
4 tablespoons kirsch
freshly ground black pepper
freshly grated nutmeg
French bread, cubed

Serves 4

To make fondue it is best if you have a dish or *caquelon*, with a small spirit burner which will keep the cheese hot for the duration of the meal.

Rub the inside of the dish with the cut clove of garlic. Pour in the wine and heat. Add the cheese, stirring constantly. In a separate dish, blend the cornflour with the kirsch. As soon as the cheese mixture begins to bubble stir in the cornflour mixture. Season with pepper and a little nutmeg. Serve the fondue in the pan in which it was cooked. Spear a cube of the French bread with a long fork and dip it into the fondue.

RÖSTI

1 kg potatoes
butter
salt and freshly ground black pepper

Serves 4–6

Put the potatoes in a saucepan of cold water, place over the heat and parboil. Drain, peel and grate the potatoes and squeeze the excess moisture from them. Heat some butter in a large heavy based frying pan, add the grated potato and season to taste. Flatten the potato with an egg slice to form a pancake and cook over a low heat until crisp and brown underneath. Turn and brown the other side. Cut into the required number of pieces.

ZÜRCHER GESCHNETZELTES   VEAL AND MUSHROOMS FROM ZÜRICH

100 g butter
1 onion, peeled and chopped
750 g veal, cut into strips (about 5 cm by 3 cm)
salt and freshly ground black pepper
¾ cup white wine
300 g mushrooms
1 cup milk
½ cup evaporated milk
1 tablespoon cornflour
2 tablespoons water

Serves 6

Heat half the butter in a pan and sauté the onion until golden. Remove and keep warm. In the same pan cook the veal over a medium heat until it is brown, adding more of the butter when necessary. Return the onion to the pan. Season with salt and pepper and add the wine. Simmer gently for 15 minutes, stirring to ensure it does not stick.

Heat the remaining butter in another pan and sauté the mushrooms for 5 minutes. Season with salt and pepper and add the two milks, stirring until the mixture is simmering. Add this to the veal mixture, stirring gently. Mix the cornflour and water in a cup until you have a smooth paste, add to the pan and continue to stir until it thickens. Serve.

ÄPFEL KUCHEN   APPLE SPONGE

1¼ cups milk
45 g semolina
125 g butter
125 g castor sugar
3 egg yolks
90 g blanched almonds
60 g seedless raisins
1 teaspoon cinnamon
250 g cooking apples
½ cup fresh white breadcrumbs
3 egg whites

Serves 6–8

Preheat the oven to 180°C/350°F and grease a 22-cm cake or ring tin.

Heat the milk in a medium-sized pan, stir in the semolina and simmer for 3 minutes, stirring constantly. Set aside to cool. In a clean bowl cream the butter and sugar until light and fluffy. Add the egg yolks, one at a time, still beating. Chop 60 g of the almonds and fold them into the semolina mixture together with the butter and sugar mixture, raisins and cinnamon. Add the chopped apples and breadcrumbs. Whisk the egg whites until stiff and fold into the cake mixture. Pour into the prepared tin, decorate with the remaining whole almonds and bake in the oven for 1¼ hours or until golden and firm. Allow to cool before serving.

MARZIPAN LECHERLI   MARZIPAN BISCUITS

250 g castor sugar
250 g ground almonds
2 tablespoons orange flower water
2 egg yolks
icing sugar
butter

Icing
1 egg white
90 g icing sugar, sifted
2 tablespoons orange flower water

Makes 24

The dough for these biscuits must stand overnight before cooking so remember to allow the extra time.

Place the sugar, ground almonds and orange flower water into a double saucepan and cook, stirring until the mixture leaves the sides of the pan. Allow to cool slightly. Add the egg yolks one at a time and mix well. Dust a surface lightly with icing sugar and roll out the mixture until it is about half a centimetre thick. Cut into small circles. Lightly butter a baking sheet, place the biscuits on it, cover and allow to stand at room temperature overnight.

Next day, preheat the oven to 180°C/350°F and cook the biscuits for 10–15 minutes. Allow to cool.

To make the icing, whisk the egg white in a bowl and fold in the icing sugar and enough orange flower water to make a smooth icing. Ice the biscuits and when set, store in an airtight tin.

A 13th-century inscription on a stone tablet in Bangkok's National Museum reads: 'In the water there is fish, in the fields there is rice'. Most Thais are still farmers, growing rice for home consumption and for export. Rice, usually steamed rather than boiled, is the main constituent of Thai meals, accompanied by various side dishes made from fish and poultry.

Fish is an important staple and like the neighbouring Burmese, the Thais often pound several ingredients into a paste to form the basis of a dish. Dried prawn paste and fish sauce are frequently used as a flavouring. Present on most meal tables are nam prik, *a hot spicy sauce made from fish, garlic, chilli and dried prawn paste and* nam pla, *the Thai equivalent of Chinese soy sauce.*

Thai food can be very hot and spicy and utilises the roots, leaves and seeds of many herbs and fruits such as coriander and limes. Chillies, dried shrimps, onions, garlic, coconut milk and fragrant lemon grass are employed individually or in combinations. Finely grated lemon rind can be used instead of lemon grass if the latter is unobtainable.

The Thais are second only to the Japanese in the importance they place upon the presentation of their food; colour is an important aspect of planning a meal and food often comes garnished with flowers.

Thai food markets reward the visitor not only with an exciting visual experience but also with many new and pungent smells. Bangkok's floating market, where food is sold from shallow-bottomed boats along a network of canals, is the country's most famous. What is by day a market at night often becomes a large open-air restaurant with many small stalls selling a wide assortment of dishes.

GAENG LIANG FAK THONG

PUMPKIN SOUP

juice of 1 lime or ½ lemon
500 g pumpkin, peeled and chopped
100 g dried shrimps
4 spring onions, including tops
2 red and 2 green chillies, seeded and chopped
1½ teaspoons shrimp paste
5½ cups coconut milk (see page 59)
fresh basil leaves for garnishing

Serves 4–6

Pour the lime juice over the pumpkin and allow to stand for ½ an hour. Using a pestle and mortar, pound the dried shrimps, spring onions, chillies and shrimp paste with a little water until you have a smooth paste. Mix the paste with the coconut milk, bring to the boil, reduce the heat and stir until all the ingredients have amalgamated. Add the pumpkin and cook over a gentle heat for 10 minutes. Season with salt, simmer until the pumpkin is tender but take care not to let it break up. Serve garnished with the basil leaves.

NAM PLA

STRONG SALTY FISH SAUCE

6 anchovy fillets or 3 teaspoons anchovy essence
2 cloves garlic, peeled and crushed
2 teaspoons soy sauce

In Thailand nam pla is made by a complex procedure of kneading shrimps and salt together. The mixture is left to dry and the liquid that drips from it forms the nam pla. While Asian food stores sell it as fish sauce, a substitute can also be made. Blend together all the ingredients to form a smooth paste. Serve as a dip with fish or vegetable dishes.

PLA PREO-WAAN

SWEET AND SOUR FISH

plain flour for dusting fish
salt and freshly ground black pepper
600 g fish fillets
2 onions, peeled and cut into eighths
60 g canned bamboo shoots, drained and chopped
1 red or green pepper, seeded and chopped
½ cup fish stock
2 tomatoes, peeled and chopped
2 fresh red or green chillies, seeded and chopped
3-cm piece fresh ginger, peeled and finely chopped
4 cloves garlic, peeled and crushed
8 cobs canned baby corn
fresh mint

Sauce
⅓ cup wine vinegar
75 g sugar
2 tablespoons soy sauce
1 teaspoon chilli powder
½ cup fish stock
2 teaspoons cornflour

Serves 4

This recipe is very hot. It may be adjusted by using only 1 chilli and ½ teaspoon of chilli powder.

Season the flour with the salt and pepper. Slice the fish into small portions and dust lightly with the flour. Leave the prepared fish to stand while preparing the sauce.

To make the sauce, place the vinegar, sugar, soy sauce, chilli powder and the stock into a pan (not aluminium). Season with a little salt, bring to the boil, stirring occasionally. Mix the cornflour to a thin paste with a little cold water, add to the mixture in the pan and stir until the sauce boils and thickens.

Put the chopped onions, bamboo shoots and pepper into another pan and add the fish stock. Bring to the boil and simmer for 5 minutes. Add the tomatoes, chillies, ginger, garlic and baby corn and simmer for another 2 minutes. Add to the sweet and sour sauce and stir to mix.

Cook the fish in hot oil, turning to brown both sides. Drain on kitchen paper and arrange on a serving dish. Spoon the hot sauce over the fish, garnish with fresh mint and serve.

JAPAN: Sunomono (Vinegared Vegetables with Seafood). See page 75.

NEUA PAD KA-PHROA

2 tablespoons soy sauce
1 tablespoon sugar
3 tablespoons coriander seeds, roasted
salt and freshly ground black pepper
750 g lean beef, cubed
1 tablespoon ghee or butter
1 onion, peeled and grated
½ cup beef stock
1 green pepper, seeded and sliced
fresh coriander for garnishing

Serves 4–6

In a bowl combine the soy sauce, sugar and coriander seeds and season with the salt and pepper. Add the cubed meat, stir to coat the pieces and leave to marinate for 1 hour.

Melt the ghee and sauté the onion until soft. Strain the meat and add to the onion in the pan and cook, stirring until the meat browns. Add the stock together with the marinade and the green pepper, cover and simmer over a gentle heat until the meat is tender. Adjust the seasoning, garnish with the fresh coriander and serve.

MEE SIAM

375 g prawns
500 g rice noodles
¼ cup oil
2 onions, peeled, chopped and pounded
½ teaspoon chilli powder
½ teaspoon sugar
¼ cabbage, shredded
4 eggs, hardboiled and chopped
juice of 2 limes

Stock
reserved prawn shells
1 small onion, peeled and sliced
2 sprigs parsley
small piece of lime or lemon rind
4 cups water

Sauce
2 tablespoons oil
1 clove garlic, peeled and crushed
½ teaspoon chilli powder
1½ tablespoons sugar
½ teaspoon salt
2½ cups prawn stock
2 tablespoons vinegar

Serves 4

Shell and de-vein the prawns, reserving the shells for the stock. Rinse the noodles under cold running water, stand in a colander and allow to drain.

To make the stock, place the prawn shells in a pan with the onion, parsley, lime rind and water. Bring to the boil and simmer gently for ½ an hour. Strain, return the stock to the pan and reduce by boiling rapidly for 10–15 minutes.

To make the sauce, heat the oil in a pan and sauté the garlic, chilli powder, sugar and salt. Gradually pour in 2½ cups of the prawn stock, stirring at the same time. Finally add the vinegar and bring the sauce to the boil. Reserve while preparing the noodles.

To prepare the noodles, heat the ¼ cup of oil and fry the pounded onion and chilli powder. Add half the prawns and all the noodles and season with salt and the sugar. Cook over a gentle heat, stirring for 5 minutes. Lastly add the shredded cabbage and cook for a few minutes (do not allow the cabbage to become soggy).

Arrange the Siamese noodles on a platter and garnish with the chopped hardboiled eggs and the remainder of the prawns. Squeeze the lime juice over the dish and serve accompanied by the sauce.

NAM PRIK

1 tablespoon dried shrimps
2 teaspoons shrimp paste
1 tablespoon fish sauce
5 cloves garlic, peeled
2 dried red chillies
2 teaspoons soft brown sugar
juice of 1 small lime or ½ lemon
1 tablespoon soy sauce

Thai dishes are often accompanied by a small plate of dipping sauce. Nam prik is the most popular of these sauces and although it is strongly flavoured, it may be modified to suit individual tastes.

Place the dried shrimps in a fine sieve and rinse thoroughly under running water. Put all the ingredients into a blender and mix until smooth. Serve as a dip with fish, chicken or vegetable dishes.

SPAIN: Sangria (Red Wine Punch). See page 107.

KHANOM SAI KAI

SAFFRON FRITTERS

These fritters have a subtle flavour and are refreshing after a spicy meal.

¾ teaspoon powdered saffron
125 g creamed coconut
¾ cup boiling water
250 g plain flour
½ teaspoon bicarbonate of soda
pinch of salt
oil for frying

Syrup
250 g white sugar
¼ cup water

Serves 6

Soak the saffron in a little hot water. Place the creamed coconut and boiling water in a pan over a gentle heat and stir until the coconut has dissolved. Allow to cool.

Sift together the flour, bicarbonate of soda and salt. Fold the sifted ingredients into the coconut mixture and stir until you have a stiff batter. The batter should be of a dropping consistency. Add the saffron and beat.

In a medium pan heat enough oil to deep fry the fritters. When hot drop the batter, a teaspoonful at a time and cook until golden. Remove with a slotted spoon and drain.

To make the syrup, stir the sugar and water over a gentle heat until the sugar has dissolved. Bring it to the boil and cook until the mixture becomes a syrup. Dip the fritters into the syrup while still warm, remove and serve.

YAM MA MUANG

SALAD OF GREEN MANGO AND APPLE

1 large green mango
salt
1 tablespoon oil
2 cloves garlic, peeled and crushed
180 g lean pork, finely sliced
6 spring onions, including tops, cut
    into pieces
1 teaspoon sugar
1 tablespoon fish sauce (see page 112)
1 tablespoon roasted peanuts, coarsely
    ground
1½ teaspoons dried prawn powder
1 large green tart apple

Serves 4–6

Peel the mango and slice finely, sprinkle with salt and allow to stand for 5 minutes. In a frying pan heat the oil and fry the garlic, mix in the pork and cook while still stirring until golden. Add the spring onions and cook for about another minute. Add the sugar, fish sauce, peanuts and prawn powder and stir to mix thoroughly. Remove from the heat and allow to cool.

Peel and slice the apple. Wash the mango slices to rid them of the salt and pat dry. Combine all the ingredients in a bowl and serve.

KHAN UM KLOK

COCONUT PANCAKES

100 g rice flour
125 g castor sugar
3 eggs
2½ cups coconut milk (see page 59)
90 g desiccated coconut
pinch of salt
pink and green food colouring
butter for frying
2 tablespoons desiccated coconut for
    garnishing

Serves 4

Mix the rice flour and sugar in a bowl, make a well in the centre and add the eggs and coconut milk and mix to a smooth batter. Beat for 5 minutes and then fold in the coconut. Divide the batter into three equal portions. Add a little salt to each and colour one pink, one green and leave the other plain. Allow the batter to stand for ½ an hour.

Lightly grease a heavy based pan and heat. Pour a thin layer of the batter in the pan and swirl it around to coat the base. Cook until the pancake is brown underneath, turn over and cook on the other side. Repeat with the rest of the batter. Roll the pancakes, garnish with desiccated coconut and serve one of each colour per person. These pancakes may be served either warm or cold.

Turkey has long been a bridge between East and West, a place where the nomadic Turks of central Asia confronted the Greeks of Byzantium, the ancient name for the city of Istanbul. Today Turkish cuisine reflects both traditions.

Much Turkish food comprises composite dishes prepared in a single pot or in small packages such as yalancı dolma (stuffed vine leaves) or börek (small pastry packets filled with meat, vegetables or cheese). These dishes reveal the nomadic heritage of the Turkish people who required food which was easy to transport and to re-heat over a camp-fire or in coals in a pit. An Iranian influence can be detected in the preparation of vegetables, some stuffed with pine nuts, rice or currants.

Spices are skilfully used to enhance rather than overpower the distinctive flavour of different dishes and these are served separately so the palate is not confused by too many tastes at once. Butter and oil are both used in the preparation of food, butter for dishes served hot and oil for food served lukewarm or cold in the Greek manner.

Turks have a very sweet tooth, a preference shown in such treats known to the West as Turkish Delight and Turkish coffee. Sweet liqueurs are made from oranges while rose petals are turned into fragrant rose-petal jam. Although predominantly a Moslem country, Turkey does produce its own beer, wines and spirits.

ÇİLBİR　　　　　　　　　　　　　　EGGS WITH YOGHURT AND GARLIC

3 tablespoons butter
2 tablespoons olive oil
750 g onions, peeled and sliced
2 teaspoons sugar
salt and freshly ground black pepper
2 tablespoons hot water
¾ cup yoghurt
1 clove garlic, peeled and crushed
¼ teaspoon paprika
4 eggs

Serves 4

Melt the butter with 1 tablespoon of the oil and cook the onions very slowly. Do not allow them to brown. After about 10 minutes add the sugar and season with salt and pepper. Add the hot water, stir, cover and cook over a gentle heat for ½ an hour, stirring occasionally.

Beat the yoghurt until smooth and stir in the crushed garlic and season with salt and pepper. Stand over a pan of hot water to warm slightly. Add the paprika to the remaining oil, stirring to mix.

When the onions have finished cooking, remove them to a serving dish and keep warm. Poach the eggs and place them on top of the onions. Spoon the yoghurt over the eggs and drizzle the oil and paprika mixture over the yoghurt.

YALANCI DOLMA　　　　　　　　　　　STUFFED VINE LEAVES

Stuffed vine leaves are served as snacks or as a first course in Turkey, Greece and the Near East. The filling varies and while minced meat is often used, sometimes the leaves are stuffed simply with rice and herbs.

30 or 40 vine leaves
1 tablespoon olive oil
1 onion, peeled and finely chopped
125 g rice
2 tablespoons currants
2 tablespoons pine nuts
1 tablespoon parsley, chopped
pinch of allspice
2 tablespoons tomato purée
salt and freshly ground black pepper
extra oil for serving
lemon juice for serving

Makes about 20

Heat the olive oil in a pan and sauté the onion for 5 minutes. Wash the rice and add it to the onion in the pan, continuing to cook and stirring so that the rice is covered by a thin film of oil. Add enough water to just cover the rice, cover with a lid and cook until the rice has absorbed all the water. Add the rest of the ingredients and stir carefully. Season with salt and pepper.

Put a teaspoon of the stuffing into the centre of each vine leaf and fold it up tightly, like a little package. You may need to use two vine leaves, depending on their elasticity. Pack the stuffed leaves tightly together (so that they do not unwrap during cooking) in the pot in which they are to be cooked. If you have more than one layer separate the layers with more vine leaves. Place a saucer or plate on top of the final layer to keep the stuffed leaves firm. Cover with water, then the lid and simmer gently for 1 hour. Allow to cool in the pot. To serve, drain the water and place the stuffed vine leaves on a serving dish. Squeeze lemon juice and trickle a little olive oil over the yalancı dolma. Serve very cold.

ŞİŞ KEBAB　　　　　　　　　　　MARINATED SKEWERED LAMB

medium-sized leg of lamb, cut into cubes
1 large onion, peeled and grated
⅓ cup olive oil
juice of 1 lemon
salt and freshly ground black pepper
2 large onions
6 bay leaves

Serves 4–6

Put the cubed lamb into a large bowl with the grated onion, olive oil and lemon juice and season with salt and pepper. Stir to mix and leave to stand for at least 2 hours, stirring from time to time. Peel the two onions and cut each one into eight pieces.

Thread the meat on skewers (allow two skewers per person), alternating with pieces of onion and adding a piece of bay leaf occasionally. Cook the kebabs over charcoal or under a hot grill, turning until ready. The lamb should remain slightly pink inside.

ETLI PILAV

olive oil for frying
750 g lamb, cut into cubes
2 onions, peeled and chopped
315 g good quality long grain rice
60 g pine nuts
60 g currants
2 tomatoes, peeled and chopped
salt and freshly ground black pepper
1 tablespoon sugar
5 cups hot stock (chicken or beef)
2 teaspoons parsley, chopped
2 teaspoons sage, chopped
½ teaspoon mixed spice
nuts fried in oil for garnishing
   (optional)

Serves 6

Heat some oil in a large pan and fry the lamb until browned. Remove the lamb and reserve. Add more oil if necessary and fry the onions until golden. Return the lamb, add the rice and nuts and fry for 5 minutes, stirring constantly. Add the currants and tomatoes and season with the salt, pepper and sugar. Pour on the hot stock, add the herbs and spices and stir to mix. Cover the pot with a clean cloth and put on the lid. Cook very slowly for 1 hour; by this time all the liquid should have been absorbed. Serve at once. If desired, the pilaff can be garnished with nuts that have been fried in a little oil.

ÇERKEZ TAVUĞU

1 large chicken
cold water
1 onion, peeled
1 sprig fresh tarragon
small bunch parsley
salt and freshly ground black pepper
2 thick slices day-old bread
250 g walnuts
3 cloves garlic, peeled and crushed
**1 cup stock reserved from cooking the
   chicken**
1 teaspoon paprika

Serves 4

Put the chicken in a large pan and cover with cold water. Add the onion, tarragon, parsley and salt and pepper. Bring to the boil and simmer gently until cooked (about 1 hour). Allow the chicken to cool a little in the water in which it has been cooked.

Remove the crusts from the bread and discard. Take a little of the chicken stock and soak the bread in it. Mince the walnuts until they are very fine (you may have to put them through the mincer two or three times). Collect the walnut oil. Put the crushed garlic into a pan with the crumbled, soaked bread. Season with salt and pepper and mix well. While stirring over a gentle heat add the walnuts and a cup of the strained chicken stock. Continue to stir until you have a smooth sauce.

Remove the chicken from the pan, skin it and cut the flesh into fine slices. Arrange the chicken on a serving dish and spoon the sauce over it. Mix the paprika with the reserved walnut oil and spoon it over the sauce. This dish is usually served lukewarm.

YOĞURTLU PATLICAN

2 large aubergines
salt
1¼ cups natural yoghurt
3 cloves garlic, peeled and crushed
1 teaspoon caraway seeds
salt and freshly ground black pepper
olive oil for frying
fresh dill for garnishing

Serves 4

Wipe the aubergines with a damp cloth, slice and sprinkle them liberally with salt. Leave them to drain in a colander for about ½ an hour. The salt will draw out the bitter juices. Rinse the aubergines under running water and pat them dry. Mix the yoghurt with the crushed garlic, caraway seeds and salt and pepper. Heat the olive oil in a pan and fry the aubergine slices, a few at a time, turning until golden and soft. Place the slices on a heated plate and spoon the sauce over them. Garnish with fresh dill.

TURKEY

FASULYE PIYAZI

HARICOT BEAN SALAD

250 g haricot beans
1 bay leaf
½ teaspoon salt
3 cloves garlic, peeled and crushed
2 tablespoons olive oil
1 tablespoon wine vinegar
½ teaspoon sugar
salt and freshly ground black pepper
juice of 1 lemon
2 tablespoons parsley, chopped

Serves 4

Soak the haricot beans overnight in cold water. Next day strain the beans, put them into a pan and cover with cold water. Add the bay leaf and salt. Simmer gently until the beans are cooked, but not broken up.

In a small bowl mix together the garlic, oil, vinegar and sugar and season with salt and pepper. Strain the beans and mix the dressing into them while they are still hot. When cool squeeze the lemon over them and garnish with the parsley.

SALATININ ZEYTIN YAĞI VE SIRKESI

SALAD DRESSING

90 g walnut pieces
2 cloves garlic, peeled
4 tablespoons dry breadcrumbs
1 cup chicken stock
salt
pinch of cayenne pepper
juice of ½ lemon
freshly chopped parsley for garnishing
freshly chopped mint for garnishing

Pound the walnuts and garlic in a pestle and mortar until they form a paste. Stir in the breadcrumbs. Add the chicken stock, stirring constantly. Season to taste with the salt, cayenne pepper and lemon juice. Dress the salad and sprinkle with the chopped parsley and mint.

LOKUM

TURKISH DELIGHT

oil (preferably almond oil)
560 g white sugar
1¾ cups water
75 g cornflour
¼ teaspoon tartaric acid
1 tablespoon rose water (available from chemists)
60 g pistachio nuts, chopped
pink food colouring
icing sugar

Grease a shallow 22 × 26-cm tin with the oil. Boil the sugar and water in a large pot for about 30–40 minutes or until it becomes syrupy. Mix the cornflour with the tartaric acid, rose water and a little cold water until a smooth paste forms.

When the syrup is ready, gradually add the cornflour mixture, stirring all the time, making sure it does not become lumpy. Boil for another 20 minutes. By this time the mixture will be thicker. Add the chopped nuts and enough colouring to make the mixture pale pink. Pour into the oiled tin. When set dust liberally with icing sugar, cut into squares and roll these into icing sugar. Store in an airtight tin in a cool place.

GÜL RECELI

This is rather exotic and a jar of it would make the perfect gift for the person who has 'everything'.

2 dozen red roses
500 g castor sugar
1 tablespoon lemon juice
1¼ cups rose water
¾ cup water

This jam takes two days to prepare. Choose fresh full blown roses and remove any damaged outer leaves. Pull off the petals and cut off the white base. Into a saucepan put the sugar, lemon juice, rose water and water and bring to the boil, stirring, and simmer until the sugar has dissolved. Put the petals in a large bowl, pour the syrup over them, cover and leave overnight. The next day simmer the petals and syrup in a saucepan over a low heat, stirring all the time until the jam thickens (about 30 minutes). To test if the jam is ready put a teaspoonful onto a clean saucer—when it has cooled slightly run your finger across it and if it forms a skin the jam is ready. Pour into jars that have been previously warmed. Seal and store until ready to use.

KAHVE

4 teaspoons Turkish coffee
4 teaspoons sugar
4 coffee cups cold water

Serves 4

Turkish coffee is very strong and very sweet and is not to everyone's liking. Ideally it should be made in individual Turkish coffee pots, but can be made equally as well in a saucepan.

Bring all the ingredients to the boil in a saucepan, remove from the heat and stir. Repeat this procedure three times. Serve while the coffee is still frothy. If using individual coffee pots, divide the ingredients by four and portion out accordingly.

Prior to the First World War, when many of the great houses in the United Kingdom still had large staffs, meals could be immense affairs. Even breakfast was a major undertaking and might have included a vast array of dishes such as porridge, sausages, kidneys, bacon, scrambled eggs, kippers, mushrooms, kedgeree, tomatoes, ham, toast and marmalade. Meals today, however, are of modest proportions, even for the well-to-do.

The United Kingdom has much rich farming country and produces superb meat, but the price is often prohibitive and beyond the means of many people. Therefore, fish and poultry tend to feature prominently in the average diet. Kippers, herrings and salmon are specialities of Scotland; they are smoked and exported world-wide.

The climate in the north and west is harsh and dishes have evolved that are warming and filling as well as economical. The Scots for example, face winter mornings with a hearty bowl of porridge while the Irish have relied on the humble potato as a staple of their diet for hundreds of years, supplemented of course with the famous stout and Irish whiskey. Welsh rarebit is a characteristically simple Welsh dish. Laverbread, made from seaweed, is another and resembles puréed spinach in appearance. It is particularly good with seafood.

The English institution of High Tea remains only slightly affected by the tides of change. Included here is a selection of dishes suitable for serving with tea.

CHESTNUT SOUP   (ENGLAND)

Chestnuts are roasted over hot coals and sold by the bag during the winter months in England. The nuts make a particularly satisfying winter soup.

60 g butter
375 g chestnuts, shelled (see page 40)
1 large onion, peeled and sliced
2 sticks celery, finely chopped
2 carrots, peeled and chopped
3 cups stock
salt and pepper
sugar
2 sprigs thyme
2 sprigs parsley
1 cup cream

Serves 6

Melt the butter in a pan with a heavy base. Add the shelled chestnuts and chopped vegetables and allow them to brown slightly, stirring from time to time. In a separate pot heat the stock and then add it to the vegetables and chestnuts. Season with salt, pepper and sugar. Add the herbs and simmer gently for about an hour. Strain the stock into a bowl. Blend the chestnuts and vegetables until smooth. Stir the stock slowly into the vegetable purée, making sure the mixture remains smooth. Simmer gently for 5 minutes. Adjust the seasoning and just before serving stir in the cream. The soup must not boil again once the cream has been added. Serve with croutons and chopped parsley.

POTTED CHEESE   (ENGLAND)

250 g Stilton
90 g butter, softened
2 teaspoons brandy
cayenne pepper

Serves 4–6

The most successful of the potted cheeses are the ones made out of the blue cheeses, for example, Stilton and Gorgonzola. Mash the cheese until crumbly and work in the softened butter until the mixture is smooth and creamy. Add the brandy and a sprinkle of cayenne pepper. Place in small pots, cover and store in the refrigerator. Serve at room temperature with toast.

HADDOCK KEDGEREE   (ENGLAND)

Kedgeree was adapted by the English living in India from the Indian dish khichri. *The original* khichri *was a mixture of lentils and rice and contained no fish. Kedgeree found its way to many English breakfast tables. It also makes an excellent dish for lunch or a light supper.*

500 g smoked haddock
2½ cups long grain rice
250 g butter
1 onion, peeled and chopped
2 teaspoons turmeric
½ teaspoon ground ginger
2 hardboiled eggs, chopped
2 tablespoons currants
salt and freshly ground pepper
chopped parsley
1 lemon

Serves 4

Cook the haddock, remove the skin and bones and flake the flesh with a fork. Cook the rice.

Melt the butter in a pan and sauté the onion until soft. Add the turmeric and ginger and stir while cooking for a few minutes. Add the fish, eggs, rice and currants and season to taste. Serve garnished with parsley and wedges of lemon.

JELLIED EELS

Jellied eel has for a long time been a favourite dish of London's East End. There are still shops and stalls in the markets selling this along with cockles, mussels and winkles.

1 eel, cleaned (500 g)
1 bay leaf
juice of 1 lemon
salt and freshly ground black pepper
water

Serves 4

Cut the eel into 5-cm lengths and put the pieces into a pan with the bay leaf and lemon juice and season with salt and pepper. Pour in enough water to just cover the eel. Place a lid on the pan and cook over a gentle heat for about 45 minutes. Put in a bowl and leave in a cool place to set.

TOAD-IN-THE-HOLE

125 g plain flour
pinch of salt
1 egg
1¼ cups milk
500 g sausages
1 tablespoon dripping

Serves 4

Preheat the oven to 220°C/425°F.

To prepare the batter, sieve the flour and salt into a bowl, make a well in the centre and drop the egg into it. Start to stir and add the milk gradually, stirring all the time with a wooden spoon until all the flour is drawn in from the sides and the mixture is smooth. Leave the batter to stand for ½ an hour. Melt the dripping in a shallow baking tin, put the sausages in and cook them for 5–10 minutes, turning frequently. Pour the batter over them, put into the preheated oven and cook for about 30 minutes or until the batter has risen and browned.

STEAK AND KIDNEY PUDDING

Traditionally, during the preparation of this pudding, the meat was tossed in flour and cooked inside the suet crust. It is much more satisfactory to cook the meat first. Accordingly, the seasoning can be adjusted before it goes into the pudding, the meat will be properly cooked and the right amount of liquid will be used.

90 g butter
2 large onions, peeled and chopped
1 kg good beef, cut into bite-sized
    pieces
500 g ox kidneys, sliced
salt and freshly ground black pepper
plain flour
250 g mushrooms, wiped with a damp
    cloth and sliced
1 cup red wine
1½ cups beef stock
bouquet garni
1 dozen oysters (optional)

Suet Crust
3 cups self-raising flour
1 level teaspoon baking powder

To cook the pudding you will need a large steamer of about 2-litre capacity, greased. Preheat the oven to 180°C/350°F.

To prepare the filling, melt some of the butter and sauté the onion until soft. Remove and reserve. Dust the beef and kidneys with the seasoned flour and brown in the remaining butter. When brown, add the mushrooms and cook lightly. Return the onion to the pan and add the wine, stock and the bouquet garni and season with salt and pepper. Cover and cook either on top of the stove over a low flame or in a moderate oven until the meat is just tender. If there appears to be a lot of liquid, strain it from the meat and reduce it by boiling rapidly until it has decreased in volume. Return it to the meat.

To make the suet crust, sift the flour, baking powder, thyme and seasoning into a bowl. Add the suet and rub into the flour with your fingertips until the mixture is crumbly. Add enough cold water to make a soft dough that is not sticky. Remove a quarter of the dough and set it to one side. Roll out the remaining dough on a floured board, fold it in half and carefully drop into the prepared steamer. Open it out and gently press the edges against the edge of the steamer. There should be a slight overlap of dough over the rim. Add the prepared meat, and the oysters if being used. Roll out the remaining dough for the top. Position the dough over the filling and secure the edges by pinching together. Moisten the edges with a little milk or water when doing this to help them stick. There should be a gap between the top of the pudding and the rim of the basin. Cut a piece of foil, larger than the top of the steamer, and fold a pleat down the centre to allow for expansion during cooking.

good pinch of dried thyme
salt and pepper
180 g fresh suet, grated
cold water

Serves 6–8

Tie the foil securely with string around the steamer and steam the pudding for $2\frac{1}{2}$ hours. Make sure that the water does not boil dry during steaming.

When ready to serve, do not turn the pudding out of the pan, but arrange a fresh white napkin around the base and serve from the dish.

JUGGED HARE   (ENGLAND)

1 hare (2–$2\frac{1}{2}$ kg)
1 bottle red wine
3 tablespoons oil
plain flour
salt and pepper
$\frac{1}{4}$ cup brandy
$2\frac{1}{2}$ cups water
2 tablespoons tomato purée
2 cloves garlic, peeled and crushed
bouquet garni
butter for frying
1 onion, chopped
250 g bacon, chopped
250 g mushrooms
$\frac{1}{2}$ cup cream
parsley for garnishing

Serves 6–8

Cut the hare into portions taking care to reserve the blood. Place the pieces of meat in a large bowl, pour over the wine and leave to marinate for 24 hours. Then remove the hare and pat dry with absorbent paper. Reserve the marinade. Heat 3 tablespoons of oil in a large pan, dust the pieces of hare with seasoned flour and brown. Warm the brandy, pour over the hare in the pan and set it alight. Add 1 cup of the marinade and $2\frac{1}{2}$ cups of water, the tomato purée, garlic and the bouquet garni. Cover and simmer for $\frac{1}{2}$ an hour.

In a separate pan melt a little butter and cook the onion until tender. Add the bacon and mushrooms and continue to cook for a further 5 minutes. Add this mixture to the hare in the pot and cook for a further $1\frac{1}{2}$ hours. The hare and its sauce will be a rich brown. In a bowl mix the reserved blood with the cream and add a few spoons of the sauce from the pot. Mix thoroughly and add to the sauce in the pan. Serve garnished with fresh sprigs of parsley.

CUMBERLAND SAUCE   (ENGLAND)

2 oranges
1 lemon
$\frac{1}{2}$ cup port
$\frac{1}{4}$ cup vinegar
1 dessertspoon French mustard
1 tablespoon castor sugar
salt and freshly ground pepper
250 g redcurrant jelly

This sauce is a traditional accompaniment to cold game, tongue and poultry. With a potato peeler remove the rind from the oranges and lemon. Cut the rind into tiny matchsticks and boil for 5 minutes in water to remove the bitter taste. Drain. Put the port, vinegar, mustard, sugar and peel into a pan. Squeeze the oranges and lemon and add the juice to the pan and season with salt and pepper. Cook over a gentle heat, slowly adding the redcurrant jelly. Simmer gently for about 20 minutes. Store in bottles and refrigerate.

SUMMER PUDDING   (ENGLAND)

sliced white bread, crusts removed
125 g castor sugar
4 cups soft summer fruit (e.g. raspberries, redcurrants, strawberries, blackcurrants)
2 tablespoons brandy
fresh fruit, citrus leaves or eau-de-cologne mint for decoration
fresh cream for serving

Serves 6

Line a basin or mould with the sliced bread, packing it so that there are no gaps between the slices. Put the sugar (you may wish to adjust the amount if the fruit is naturally sweet), fruit and brandy into a pan and stir carefully over a gentle heat until the sugar dissolves. Allow to cool. Spoon half the fruit mixture into the prepared basin and cover with a layer of bread. Add the remainder of the fruit and cover with another layer of bread. Choose a plate that fits snugly into the top of the bowl, seal with this and top with a heavy weight. Allow to stand in the refrigerator overnight. To serve, carefully remove the pudding from the basin and invert it onto a serving plate. If desired it can be decorated around the base with fresh fruit and citrus leaves or eau-de-cologne mint. Serve with fresh cream.

BREAD AND BUTTER PUDDING

(ENGLAND)

butter for spreading
10 slices white bread, crusts removed
1 cup sultanas
3 tablespoons sugar
6 egg yolks
4 egg whites
2½ cups milk
freshly grated nutmeg
½ teaspoon cinnamon
½ cup peach, plum or apricot jam,
    heated and strained

Serves 6

Preheat the oven to 180°C/350°F.

Butter the bread and cut it into fingers. Arrange half of these, buttered side up, in an ovenproof dish. Add the sultanas, sprinkle with sugar and cover with the remaining bread fingers.

Whisk the egg yolks and whites in a bowl with the milk and add the cinnamon. Pour onto the bread and grate the nutmeg over the top. Place the baking dish in a pan of cold water and bake in a moderate oven until the bread is golden and the custard has set—about 45 minutes. Spoon the heated jam over the top and serve warm.

SYLLABUB

(ENGLAND)

rind of 1 lemon, finely grated
juice of 1 lemon
½ cup sherry
2 tablespoons brandy
60 g castor sugar
1½ cups cream
freshly grated nutmeg
small sprigs of rosemary or crystallized
    violets for decoration

Serves 4

The syllabub is, unlike many other traditional English sweets, light and delicate as well as being easy to prepare. You will need to start preparation the day before use.

Put the finely grated rind and juice of a lemon in a bowl with the sherry and brandy. Leave overnight.

The next day strain the wine and lemon liquid into a deep bowl and stir in the castor sugar. Keep stirring until it has all dissolved. Now add the cream, stirring all the time. Add a little freshly grated nutmeg and whisk the mixture until it thickens. It is best to do this by hand with a wire whisk, although an electric mixer can be used. When the syllabub has reached the right consistency (similar to whipped cream), spoon it into small glasses. If you wish they can be decorated with small sprigs of rosemary or crystallized violets. Store in a cool place (*not* in the refrigerator) until ready to serve.

IRISH STEW

(IRELAND)

1 kg best end neck of mutton
1 kg potatoes, peeled and sliced
2 medium onions, peeled and sliced
    into rings
salt and freshly ground black pepper
2½ cups stock
freshly chopped parsley

Serves 4

First cut the meat into cutlets, removing as much fat as possible. Choose a large pot and put a layer of potatoes and onions in the bottom. Season with salt and pepper. Now place the chops over the potatoes and onions. Season again. Add another layer of potatoes and onions and season. Pour over the stock and simmer until the meat is tender—about 1½ hours. Sprinkle with parsley and serve.

POTATO BREAD

(IRELAND)

750 g potatoes of uniform size
1 teaspoon salt
1 tablespoon melted butter
flour plain
extra butter

Wash the potatoes thoroughly and then steam them in their skins until tender. When the potatoes have cooled, peel and mash until they are free of any lumps. Add the salt and melted butter and then sift in enough flour to make a pliable dough. Knead well on a lightly floured board for about 5 minutes. Roll out the dough to a 1.3-cm thickness and cut it into

Serves 4–6

circles. Grease a heavy based pan and place on the stove. Cook the rounds of potato bread until browned. Turn the bread over and cook on the other side and serve hot with butter.

IRISH COFFEE (IRELAND)

6 teaspoons castor sugar
4 cups strong black coffee, freshly brewed
¾ cup Irish whiskey
½ cup whipped cream

Serves 4

Warm 4 glasses. Dissolve the sugar in the hot coffee, pour it into the glasses and add 1½ tablespoons of whiskey to each glass and stir. Top with whipped cream and serve at once.

QUEEN OF SCOTS SOUP (SCOTLAND)

250 g sorrel leaves
90 g butter
250 g potatoes, peeled and cooked
1.5 litres chicken stock
salt and freshly ground pepper
¾ cup cream

Serves 4–6

Remove the stalks from the sorrel and wash the leaves. Melt the butter and gently cook the sorrel leaves until they wilt. Add the potato and chicken stock, season with salt and pepper and simmer gently for 45 minutes. Allow to cool slightly and then blend until smooth. Reheat the soup, add the cream and check the seasoning. Do not allow the soup to boil after the cream has been added. The soup can be garnished with whipped cream before serving.

COCK-A-LEEKIE SOUP (SCOTLAND)

This hearty soup is really a meal in itself. It is best if it is made 24 hours beforehand and re-heated just before serving.

4 large leeks
500 g shin of beef
1 medium-sized boiling fowl
bouquet garni (1 bay leaf, 1 sprig parsley, 1 sprig thyme)
salt and freshly ground black pepper
125 g prunes

Serves 6–8

Wash the leeks carefully, remove the green tops and any tough outer leaves and cut into thin slices. Cut the beef into small pieces. Wipe the fowl inside and out with a damp cloth. In a large pan put the beef, fowl, chopped leeks and bouquet of herbs, cover with cold water and season with salt and pepper. Bring to the boil and simmer gently for 3 hours (or until the chicken meat pulls away easily from the bones). Skim any scum from the pan during the cooking. It may be necessary to top up the water during this time. Add the prunes and simmer for another 45 minutes. Remove the fowl and allow to cool slightly. Remove the skin and chop the meat into small pieces, removing any sinews and bones. Return to the pan, adjust the seasoning and bring back to simmering point. Serve in a large tureen.

BLOATER PASTE (SCOTLAND)

4 herrings
60 g butter, softened
1 teaspoon anchovy essence
pinch of cayenne pepper
1 bay leaf
salt and freshly ground black pepper

Serves 4–6

Clean the herrings, place them in a pan with the bay leaf and cover with cold water. Bring to the boil and simmer for 10 minutes. Remove the herrings from the pan and allow to cool slightly. Cut off the heads and remove the skin and bones. Pound the fish in a pestle and mortar with the softened butter, anchovy essence and cayenne pepper, until you have a smooth paste. If necessary add a little more butter. Season to taste with salt and pepper. Put into small jars, cover and refrigerate until ready to use. Serve with toast.

SCOTCH WOODCOCK

(SCOTLAND)

8 anchovy fillets
1 tablespoon butter
freshly ground pepper
4 slices of toast, crusts removed
4 egg yolks
1 cup cream
1 tablespoon chopped parsley
pinch of cayenne pepper

Serves 4

Mash the anchovy fillets with the butter until you have a smooth paste. Season with pepper. Spread this mixture thinly on the pieces of toast and keep warm. Beat the egg yolks in a double boiler and add the cream, parsley and cayenne. Stir over boiling water until the mixture is thick. Pour over the toast and serve.

ROAST PHEASANT

(SCOTLAND)

1 pheasant (about 850 g)
1 large tablespoon butter
plain flour for the gravy

Bread Sauce
1½ cups milk
1 small onion
4 cloves
1 small bay leaf
1 tablespoon butter
salt and white pepper
1 very thick slice of white bread or 3
  slices sandwich bread, crusts
  removed

Serves 4

Eliza Acton in her book *Modern Cookery for Private Families*, first published in 1845, gives some hints on cooking pheasants: 'Unless kept to the proper point, a pheasant is one of the most tough, dry, and flavourless birds that is sent to table; but when it has hung as many days as it can without becoming really tainted, and is well roasted and served, it is most excellent eating. Pluck off the feathers carefully, cut a slit in the back of the neck to remove the crop, then draw the bird in the usual way, and either wipe the inside very clean with a damp cloth, or pour water through it; wipe the outside also, but with a dry cloth; cut off the toes, turn the head of the bird *under* the wing, with the bill laid straight along the breast, skewer the legs, which must not be crossed, flour the pheasant well, lay it to a brisk fire, and baste it constantly and plentifully with well flavoured butter. Send bread-sauce and good brown gravy to table with it. When a brace is served, one is sometimes larded, and the other not; but a much handsomer appearance is given to the dish by larding both. About ¾ an hour will roast them, ¾ an hour; a few minutes less, if liked very much underdone; five or ten more for *thorough* roasting, with a *good* fire in both cases'.

Today's pheasants can still be tough and dry and care must be taken with the cooking to avoid this. Preheat the oven to 190°C/375°F.

Choose a young bird, dressed and drawn. Put a good tablespoon of butter inside the bird. Generously butter a sheet of foil large enough to wrap around the bird. When the bird has been securely wrapped, place it on its side on a rack in a baking tin. Place in the preheated oven for 20 minutes and then turn the bird onto its other side and cook for another 15 minutes. Remove the foil, turn the bird breast facing upwards and cook for a further 10–15 minutes. Remove and keep warm.

While the pheasant is cooking, make the bread sauce. Place the milk into a small pan. Cut the onion in two and stick two cloves into each half. Add the onion and cloves to the milk along with the bay leaf. Bring to the boil slowly, draw the pan from the heat, cover and allow to stand for half an hour. Add the butter, season with salt and pepper and tear the bread into pieces and add to the pan. Return to the stove and cook over a very low heat for a further 20 minutes. Remove the bay leaf and onion and stir the sauce with a wooden spoon to break up the bread—it should not be lumpy nor too smooth. Before serving whisk the sauce with a fork and adjust the seasoning.

To make the gravy, add a little flour to the scrapings in the pan, heat and add water. Stir constantly until the gravy thickens.

SCOTCH EGGS   (SCOTLAND)

When making this dish it is best to use free-range eggs and good quality sausage meat.

6 eggs, hardboiled
salt and freshly ground black pepper
plain flour
750 g sausage meat
1 egg, beaten
fresh white breadcrumbs
oil for frying

Serves 6

Carefully shell the eggs and roll in seasoned flour. Divide the sausage meat into 6 equal portions and pat each portion out flat. Place an egg in the centre of one portion of meat and work the meat around the egg, to completely enclose it. Roll the meat in the beaten egg and then in the breadcrumbs. Repeat the procedure until the six eggs have been wrapped and crumbed. Allow the Scotch eggs to stand in the refrigerator for $\frac{1}{2}$ an hour. Heat some oil in a pan and deep fry the eggs until golden. They can be served while still warm or cold.

STOVED CHICKEN   (SCOTLAND)

1 fresh chicken (about 1$\frac{1}{2}$ kg)
2 tablespoons butter
1.5 kg potatoes, peeled and thickly sliced
12 small whole shallots or 2 large onions, peeled and sliced
salt and freshly ground pepper
2 cups chicken stock
freshly chopped parsley

Serves 4

Cut the chicken into bite-sized pieces and place in a pan with melted butter to brown. In an earthenware casserole place a layer of the sliced potatoes, then a layer of the shallots, seasoning each layer with salt and pepper. Add a layer of the chicken. Continue in this way until all the chicken and vegetables have been used, ending with a layer of potatoes. Pour any remaining butter over the potatoes. Now pour the stock into the dish and cover with a piece of buttered paper and then a lid. Cook in a slow oven at 150°C/300°F for about 1$\frac{1}{2}$ hours or until the chicken is tender. Sprinkle with chopped parsley and serve.

MULLED CIDER PUNCH   (SCOTLAND)

2 apples
4 cloves
1 cinnamon stick, about 8 cm long
2 teaspoons ground ginger
2 tablespoons soft brown sugar
$\frac{3}{4}$ cup water
2 extra cloves
1 orange, thinly sliced
1 bottle cider

Draught cider from the West Country has an incredible 'kick' and many have been caught unawares. The bottled variety is less potent and makes a pleasant alternative to beer or wine.
Preheat the oven to 180°C/350°F.
Remove the core from the apples and scrape away a little of the peel from around the ends. Stick each apple with 2 cloves. Bake the apples in a moderate oven for $\frac{1}{2}$ an hour.
Place the cinnamon stick, ginger, sugar, water and extra cloves into a pan. Cook over a gentle heat until the sugar dissolves, bring to the boil and simmer for 5 minutes. Add the orange slices, remove the pan from the heat and allow to stand.
When the apples are cooked, remove them from the oven and allow them to cool enough to handle. Cut each apple into pieces, without removing the skin. Place the pieces in the bottom of a large jug or punch bowl. Warm the cider and add to the jug. Strain in the spiced punch water. Serve while hot.

OATCAKES

I have special childhood memories of visits from my Scottish grandfather, when a batch of oatcakes would invariably appear. Oatcakes are equally good with savoury or sweet things; for example they can be served with herrings and raw onions or butter and marmalade.

⅔ **cup medium oatmeal**
pinch of salt
pinch of bicarbonate of soda
2 teaspoons fat, melted
¼ **cup hot water**
extra oatmeal for kneading

Makes 4 cakes

Place the oatmeal, salt and bicarbonate of soda in a basin and make a well in the centre. Add the melted fat, stir and add the water until you have a stiff paste. Sprinkle some oatmeal onto a board and roll the paste into a ball. Knead the paste, adding more oatmeal if the mixture becomes too sticky. Roll out to about a 6-mm thickness, place a plate over the top and cut round the plate so that a smooth edge is acquired. Now cut the oatcakes into quarters. Preheat a lightly greased pan on the stove, put in the four oatcakes and cook over a gentle heat for 6–8 minutes, turning to cook evenly on both sides.

DUNDEE CAKE

---

250 g butter at room temperature
250 g soft brown sugar
4 eggs
315 g plain flour
125 g currants
125 g raisins
125 g sultanas
125 g candied peel, chopped
60 g whole almonds
rind of 1 orange, finely grated
rind of 1 lemon, finely grated

Serves 8–10

Preheat the oven to 150°C/300°F and grease a 22-cm cake tin.

Cream the butter and sugar until light and then add the eggs, one at a time, beating continuously. Sift a little of the flour into the mixture and fold in a little of the fruit (it is best to do this by hand as beating the cake once the flour has been added makes it tough). Continue slowly adding the flour and fruit in this manner (reserve a few almonds for decoration). Put the mixture into the prepared tin and decorate with the remaining almonds. Bake for 2½–3 hours. When quite firm remove the cake from the oven and allow to cool completely before cutting.

DUNDEE MARMALADE

According to legend a ship travelling from Spain in the early 18th century took refuge from a storm in Dundee harbour. Seville oranges were part of its cargo and were bought rather cheaply by one of Dundee's local inhabitants. Unable to sell them because of their bitterness, the shrewd person in question made them into a conserve which today is famous the world over.

1 kg Seville or other bitter oranges
2 lemons
8 cups water
2 kg granulated sugar

Makes 3 kg marmalade

Wash the fruit and put it into a large pan, add the water, cover and simmer for about 1½ hours or until the skin of the fruit is easy to pierce. Remove the fruit and allow to cool. Leave the water in the pan. With a sharp knife cut the fruit to the thickness required (this marmalade is traditionally coarsely cut). Take care to retain any pips and add these to the water in the pan. Boil the water for 10 minutes and then strain off the pips. Add the chopped fruit and bring to the boil. Add the sugar and stir with a wooden spoon over a gentle heat until the sugar has dissolved. Then boil constantly without stirring until a setting point has been reached (about ½ an hour). To test the marmalade, place a teaspoonful onto a clean saucer and allow to cool slightly. If the marmalade wrinkles when a finger is pushed through it, the jam is ready. Pour into warm sterilized jars and cover at once.

UNITED KINGDOM: Tea selection. Dundee Cake (see this page), Shortbread (see page 129) and Caerphilly Scones (see page 129).

SHORTBREAD

250 g plain flour
125 g cornflour
120 g castor sugar
250 g unsalted butter

Serves 6

Preheat the oven to 160°C/325°F and grease a baking sheet.
 Sift the plain flour and cornflour into a bowl. Add the sugar and then rub in the butter. Turn the dough onto a lightly floured board and knead lightly. Roll the mixture out to a thickness of about 5 cm and prick all over with a fork. Bake in the oven for about 30 minutes or until cooked. Do not allow the shortbread to brown. Allow to cool for 10 minutes before cutting into pieces. When cool store in an airtight tin.

FFAGODAU

1 kg liver (pig, lamb or ox)
2 onions, peeled
90 g suet
125 g fresh white breadcrumbs
2 teaspoons chopped fresh sage
salt and freshly ground black pepper
1 tablespoon plain flour

Serves 4–6

Preheat the oven to 180°C/350°F and grease an ovenproof dish.
 Rinse the liver under a cold tap and then dry. Mince the liver, onion and suet. Add the breadcrumbs and chopped sage and season with salt and pepper. Mix thoroughly and form into small balls and place in the prepared dish. Cover and cook in a moderate oven for about 40 minutes. Remove the lid 10 minutes before the end of the cooking time to allow the faggots to brown. When ready, remove the faggots from the dish and keep warm. Make the gravy by adding the flour to the juices in the pan. Add hot water or stock and stir until boiling. Season and serve.

SGONAU CAERFFILI

250 g self-raising flour
pinch of salt
45 g butter
60 g Caerphilly cheese, grated
45 g castor sugar
150 ml milk

Makes 10–12 scones

Preheat the oven to 220°C/425°F. Sift the flour and salt into a bowl and rub the butter in with your fingertips. Add the grated cheese and the sugar. Slowly add enough milk to make a soft dough. Turn out onto a floured board and roll out until it is about 2 cm thick. Cut into rounds and place on an ungreased baking tray. Brush with a little milk and cook in the preheated oven for about 10 minutes, or until the scones have risen and are golden in colour.

CEULED LEMYN

4 lemons, washed and dried
5 eggs
125 g butter
500 g sugar

Grate the lemon rind on the finest blade of the grater and squeeze the juice from the lemons. Break the eggs into a bowl and beat until light. Add the lemon juice, rind, butter and sugar and place in the top of a double boiler over simmering water. Cook, stirring constantly until the curd thickens. Have ready small sterilised jars (it is best if they are warm—they will not crack when the hot lemon mixture is poured into them). When the mixture is ready, strain into the prepared jars and seal immediately. Refrigerate when cool.

TURKEY: Lokum (Turkish Delight). See page 118.

To speak of American food may be to conjure up images of mass produced 'fast food' but there are in fact, many splendid traditional American dishes, introduced by immigrants from all parts of the globe and adapted to suit local conditions.

Americans still sit down to a Thanksgiving dinner of roast turkey with chestnut stuffing, sweet potatoes, corn and cranberry sauce, commemorating the original giving of thanks by the Pilgrim Fathers for their safe arrival in the New World.

The clambake is another American favourite. Seaweed is spread over hot rocks, and lobsters, green maize and clams are added in layers. After cooking the feast begins, starting with the top layer of clams, followed by the maize and finished with the lobsters, all cooked to perfection!

There is a great diversity of food between the different states due to geographic and climatic variations and the influence of neighbouring peoples. This is particularly evident in those states adjacent to Mexico, where local cuisine can have a distinctly Spanish flavour.

Americans invented the cocktail and their preference tends to be for 'mixed drinks'. American whiskey or 'Bourbon' is made from maize and is stronger than its Scottish counterpart.

PUMPKIN SOUP

60 g butter
2 cups cooked mashed pumpkin
1 teaspoon brown sugar
salt and freshly ground pepper
3 cups milk
1 cup cream
croutons for serving

Serves 4

Melt the butter in a medium-sized pan and add the pumpkin and sugar. Season to taste with the salt and pepper and cook over a gentle heat for about 5 minutes. Heat the milk and stir gradually into the pumpkin mixture, taking care that no lumps form. Lastly add the cream, stirring constantly. Do not let the soup boil after the addition of the cream. Adjust the seasoning and serve with croutons. These can be made by cutting the crusts from 3 slices of day-old bread and dicing the bread into small cubes. Heat 2 tablespoons of oil and 1 tablespoon of butter in a small pan and fry the cubed bread, turning until golden on all sides. Drain on absorbent paper.

CHILE CON CARNE

This dish has its origins in the American southwest, not Mexico as is often thought.

250 g red kidney beans
2 tablespoons oil
1 onion, peeled and chopped
1 teaspoon cummin
1 teaspoon oregano
1 red chilli, seeded and chopped
½ teaspoon chilli powder
dash of Tabasco
500 g minced beef
400 g canned tomatoes

Serves 4–6

You need to start the preparation of this dish the day before: cover the beans in cold water and leave them to soak overnight. The next day drain the beans and place in a pan. Cover with fresh water, bring to the boil and simmer gently until almost tender. Drain and reserve.

Heat the oil in a deep frying pan and sauté the onion until lightly browned. Add the cummin, oregano, chilli, chilli powder (this is a fiery dish and you may wish to omit either the chilli or the chilli powder) and Tabasco. Stir while cooking for 2 minutes. Add the beef, stir and brown lightly. Add the tomatoes and the beans, cover and simmer gently for 15–20 minutes. Serve.

BOSTON BAKED BEANS

This dish had its origins in Puritan times. The Sabbath lasted from sundown on Saturday until sundown on Sunday and the beans could be prepared in advance and kept warm in front of the fireplace.

3 cups haricot beans
1 teaspoon salt
500 g belly of pork, chopped
½ cup molasses
1 dessertspoon dry English mustard
1 teaspoon extra salt
freshly ground pepper
1 onion peeled

Serves 4–6

You will need to start the preparation of this dish the day before. Place the beans in a bowl, cover with cold water and leave them to soak overnight. The next day drain the beans, place them in a pan and cover with fresh cold water. Add the teaspoon of salt and bring to the boil. Lower the heat and simmer gently. The beans are cooked when the skins start to wrinkle and burst. Drain off the liquid.

Heat a large frying pan and brown the chopped pork (there is sufficient fat in the pork to do this). Mix the molasses with the mustard and the extra salt and season with freshly ground pepper.

In an earthenware pot place alternate layers of the beans, the molasses mixture and the chopped pork. Bury the onion in the middle of the beans. When the pot is nearly full, cover with boiling water and place a lid on top. Bake in a very slow oven at 120°C/250°F. Check occasionally to see that the water has not dried up and if necessary top up with more water. This dish should cook for up to 6 hours. During the last hour of cooking remove the lid so that the top can become crisp.

OYSTER STEW

2 cups milk
2 cups cream
24 oysters and their liquid
30 g butter
celery salt
white pepper
paprika

Serves 4

Choose the bowls that are to be used to serve the stew and warm them. Heat the milk and cream together, but do not allow the mixture to boil. Drain the liquid from the oysters into a separate pan and bring to the boil. Place the oysters in another pan with a little of their warmed liquid and the butter and heat until they become plump. Remove the oysters from the heat and combine with the hot oyster liquid and the milk and cream. Season with the celery salt and pepper and serve in the heated bowls sprinkled with paprika.

NEW ENGLAND BOILED DINNER

2 kg corned beef
6 medium potatoes, peeled
6 carrots, scraped
1 large swede, peeled and cut into six
    pieces
1 cabbage, cut into six pieces
1 small marrow, seeds and membrane
    removed, cut into chunks

Serves 6–8

Place the meat in a large pot and cover with water and bring to the boil. Reduce the heat and simmer gently for 3–3½ hours or until tender. About ½ an hour before the meat is ready add the whole potatoes, whole carrots and the pieces of swede. Increase the heat so that the broth continues to simmer. About 15 minutes later add the cabbage and marrow. Increase the heat again if necessary—to retain simmering point. Serve the meat on a large meat platter surrounded by the vegetables.

CAESAR SALAD

2 tablespoons butter
1 clove garlic, peeled and crushed
3 slices bread, crusts removed and
    diced
6 tablespoons grated Parmesan
1 cos lettuce, washed, dried and torn
    into pieces
2 egg yolks, beaten
croutons for garnishing
6 flat anchovy fillets

Dressing
6 tablespoons olive oil
2 tablespoons wine vinegar
1 clove garlic, peeled and crushed
salt and freshly ground black pepper

Serves 4–6

Heat the butter in a small pan, sauté the garlic and then add the diced bread. Turn until it is golden on all sides. Remove and drain on absorbent paper.

To make the dressing, combine the olive oil, wine vinegar and garlic. Mix well and season with salt and pepper.

Toss the Parmesan with the lettuce, add the dressing and toss lightly. Add the beaten egg yolks and carefully mix so that every leaf is coated with the egg mixture. Garnish with croutons (see pumpkin soup recipe, page 131) and anchovies and serve.

WALDORF SALAD

This famous salad takes its name from the hotel where it was first served, The Waldorf Astoria in New York city.

Core and dice the apples, but leave the skin on. Wash and chop the celery. Add the mayonnaise to the apple and celery and toss to mix thoroughly. Arrange the lettuce in the bottom of a bowl so that the

2 large apples
2 sticks celery
6 leaves cos lettuce
2 tablespoons mayonnaise
2 tablespoons walnuts, chopped

Serves 4

leaves come up the sides, fill the bowl with the apple and celery mixture and garnish with the chopped walnuts.

PUMPKIN PIE

Pumpkin pie is an American favourite. It can be served with a slice of good Cheddar cheese, or if preferred, with whipped cream and a little crystallized ginger.

2 cups cooked pumpkin
⅔ cup brown sugar, firmly packed
2 teaspoons cinnamon
½ teaspoon ground ginger
½ teaspoon salt
¾ cup milk
2 eggs, well beaten
1 cup of cream
¼ cup of brandy

Rich Shortcrust Pastry
250 g plain flour
pinch of salt
1 teaspoon sugar
125 g butter
1 egg yolk
3 tablespoons iced water

To make the pastry, first grease a 22-cm pie plate. Sift the flour, salt and sugar into a bowl. Rub in the butter until it looks like fine breadcrumbs. Beat the yolk with the water and add to the mixture. Mix to form a firm dough. It should not be too sticky. If necessary add a little more water or flour. Roll out, line the pie plate, prick the base and allow to rest in the refrigerator for ½ an hour before using.

Preheat the oven to 180°C/350°F.

In a large bowl, mix the pumpkin, sugar, spices and salt. Make sure there are no lumps in the pumpkin. Beat continuously while adding the milk, eggs, cream and brandy. Pour into the unbaked pastry shell and bake in the preheated moderate oven for 1 hour. Serve cold with Cheddar cheese or whipped cream.

PECAN ICE CREAM

The pecan nut, a native of North America, was used as a source of nutrition by many American Indians during the winter months. Pecans resemble walnuts, although the shell is smooth, and they can be successfully substituted in recipes requiring walnuts.

1 cup pecan nuts
60 g butter
2 cups light brown sugar, lightly packed
1 cup water
good pinch of salt
4 eggs
2 teaspoons vanilla essence
1 liqueur glass sherry
1 litre milk
1 litre cream

Serves 10–12

Chop the pecans into pieces. Melt the butter in a small pan and cook the nuts until the butter foams. Add the sugar, water and salt and bring to the boil. Simmer for 2 minutes. In a bowl, beat the eggs until light and then add a little of the hot syrup from the pan and mix well. Place the beaten egg mixture and the nut syrup mixture in the top of a double boiler over simmering water. Cook the mixture, stirring often until it thickens. Take care not to let it boil. Allow to cool and then add the remaining ingredients and mix thoroughly. Place in shallow trays and freeze. When almost set, remove from the freezer and beat until smooth. Return to the freezer and re-freeze.

PECAN NUT TOFFEE

1½ cups pecan nuts, chopped
2 cups sugar
2 dessertspoons lemon juice

Grease a shallow rectangular cake tin. In a separate baking tin, spread the nuts in a single layer and toast in a moderate oven at 180°C/350°F for about 10 minutes. In a heavy pan combine the sugar and lemon juice and cook over a low heat, stirring constantly until the liquid turns a golden colour. Quickly stir in the toasted pecans, and pour into the greased tin. When cool and solid, break the toffee into pieces.

BROWNIES

60 g unsweetened chocolate
125 g butter
1 cup sugar
2 eggs, beaten
1 teaspoon vanilla
½ cup plain flour, sifted
pinch of salt
½ cup walnuts, chopped

Makes about 12 brownies

Preheat the oven to 180°C/350°F and grease a 20-cm-square shallow cake tin.

Melt the chocolate in a bowl over hot water. Beat the butter until soft, add the sugar and beat until smooth. Beat in the eggs and vanilla. Fold in the sifted flour, salt, melted chocolate and chopped nuts. Pour into the prepared tin and bake in the preheated oven for 35–40 minutes. The slice should remain soft. Cut into squares.

CHRISTMAS CAKE

125 g butter
1 cup castor sugar
2 eggs
1 teaspoon vanilla essence
250 g plain flour
3 teaspoons baking powder
½ teaspoon salt
¾ cup milk
1½ tablespoons golden syrup
¾ teaspoon cinnamon
¼ teaspoon ground cloves
¼ teaspoon nutmeg
60 g walnuts, chopped

Filling
250 g marshmallows

Frosting
1½ cups brown sugar
1 cup castor sugar
pinch of salt
1½ cups coffee, made with milk
2½ tablespoons butter

Serves 8–10

American Christmas cakes differ from our traditional dark fruit cakes. They are usually a light mixture, with the addition of spices, nuts and frosting.

Preheat the oven to 180°C/350°F and grease a 20-cm cake tin.

Beat the butter and sugar in a bowl until light and fluffy. Add the eggs, one at a time and then add the vanilla. Sift the flour, baking powder and salt and fold into the mixture with the milk. Blend well, but do not beat (the cake will be tough if you beat it after the addition of the flour). Divide the batter in two. Stir the golden syrup and spices into one portion and the chopped walnuts into the other. Spoon the batters alternately into the prepared tin and bake in the preheated oven for one hour, or until a skewer, when inserted into the cake, comes away clean. Allow to cool. Split the cake in half, and spread the marshmallows on the lower half. Put under a preheated grill just long enough to melt the marshmallows. Sandwich the cake together.

To make the frosting, mix the brown sugar with the castor sugar, salt and milk coffee in a saucepan. Stir over a low heat until the sugar has dissolved. Bring to the boil, stirring all the time. Continue to boil, still stirring, until a little of the mixture forms a soft ball when dropped into cold water. Remove from the heat and stir in the butter. When almost cool, beat until the frosting begins to stiffen. Spread it quickly over the cake.

Y U G O S L A V I A

The food of Yugoslavia reflects the tastes of a people who are peasant in origin. Breakfast, for example, may consist of burek or minced meat wrapped in thin pastry, a dish of hot peppers and lots of black coffee, providing the strength required for a hard day's work. The cuisine has been influenced by that of several other countries. From Hungary come dumplings and the use of paprika to flavour fish, meat and vegetables; kebabs were introduced from Turkey; polenta from Italy; and aromatic fish stews from Greece. Yugoslavs do wonderful things with fish; sautéd in olive oil with garlic and herbs, charcoal grilled or served in delicious soups and stews, its freshness is always guaranteed.

Typical of Yugoslav food are ćevapčići, small rissoles made from ground meat and cooked over charcoal. Smoked ham, similar to Italian prosciutto, cheese, salami, spiced sausages, pickled cucumbers and peppers are also common, depending on what is available in the markets. Yoghurt is popular and the longevity of some peasants in country areas is often attributed to their consumption of this and garlic in large quantities.

Bread is a staple item of diet and comes in many varieties. On special occasions rich cakes are made with puréed chestnuts and chocolate while strudels containing chestnuts and fresh fruit reveal an Austrian influence. Liqueurs made from local fruits are drunk in copious amounts.

TARATOR SUPA

CUCUMBER SOUP

125 g walnuts, shelled
5 cloves garlic, peeled
2 tablespoons olive oil
5 cups natural yoghurt
1 cucumber, peeled and seeded
½ cup iced water
salt and freshly ground black pepper
fresh parsley or dill, chopped

Serves 6

Pound the walnuts and garlic together and add the olive oil a few drops at a time, as for a mayonnaise. When smooth add the yoghurt and beat well. Cut the cucumber into thin strips and add with the iced water. Season to taste with salt and pepper. Serve chilled, garnished with parsley or dill.

ŠARAN NA BELOM LUKA

BREAM WITH GARLIC AND PARSLEY

small bunch parsley
1 stick celery, including tops
5 cloves garlic, peeled and crushed
1 cup olive oil
juice of ½ lemon
salt and freshly ground black
    pepper
1 bream (1 kg), cleaned and scaled
¾ cup water

Serves 4

Preheat the oven to 180°C/350°F and lightly oil an ovenproof dish.

Chop the parsley and celery and add the garlic, olive oil and lemon juice. Season with salt and pepper. Rinse the fish and with a sharp knife make deep diagonal cuts on one side. Stuff the fish with some of the parsley and celery mixture, place it in the prepared dish and place the remainder of the parsley and celery mixture over the top side of the fish which has been slashed. Pour the water around the fish and bake in a moderate oven. The fish will pull away from the bone easily after about 40 minutes.

JOGURT TAVA

LAMB FROM SERBIA

1 large shoulder or forequarter of lamb
salt and freshly ground black pepper
oil
5 egg yolks
3½ cups natural yoghurt
1 teaspoon paprika
5 egg whites

Serves 4–6

Preheat the oven to 180°C/350°F.

Season the lamb with salt and pepper and put it into an oiled baking dish. Roast the meat in a moderate oven until tender, basting from time to time. (This will probably take 1½–2 hours, depending on the size of the lamb. To test if the meat is done, insert a skewer; when the juices run clear the meat is cooked.)

While the meat is cooking, beat the egg yolks and blend with the yoghurt and season with salt, pepper and paprika. When the meat is almost ready whisk the egg whites until stiff and fold into the yoghurt mixture. Pour over the meat and return to the oven until the sauce thickens.

ĆEVAPČIĆI

GRILLED MEAT BALLS

1.5 kg minced pork (neck preferably)
500 g minced topside
2 dessertspoons vegeta* or 3 crumbled
    stock cubes
1 tablespoon white pepper
3 cloves garlic, peeled and crushed
chopped onion for serving

Serves 4–6

You will need to start preparing the meat balls the day before they are required. Place all the ingredients into a large bowl, mix well, cover and store in the refrigerator overnight. Make the mixture into rolls about 8 cm long (you should get about 25 to the kilogram). Grill or barbecue until cooked. Serve with chopped raw onion.

* Special Yugoslav spice available at specialist stores.

BRODET NA DALMATINSKI NAČIN

½ cup olive oil
2 large onions, peeled and sliced
4 tablespoons tomato paste
⅓ cup hot water
1¼ kg assorted fish, cut into pieces
250 g prawns, peeled and de-veined
4 tablespoons wine vinegar
1½ cups red wine
salt and freshly ground black pepper
4 tablespoons parsley, chopped
3 cloves garlic, peeled and crushed
grated rind of ½ lemon

Serves 4

In a large pan heat the oil and sauté the onions until soft. Dilute the tomato paste in the hot water and stir into the onions. Add the fish pieces and continue to cook, shaking the pan from time to time to ensure the fish does not stick. Add the prawns, vinegar, red wine and season with salt and pepper. Top up with hot water to just cover the fish. Cook gently until the fish flakes easily. Sprinkle with the parsley, garlic and lemon rind and serve immediately.

GYUVETSCH

250 g stewing pork
250 g beef
250 g mutton
3 tablespoons oil
2 cups rice
salt and freshly ground black pepper
1 tablespoon paprika
1 bay leaf
4 onions, peeled and sliced
1 carrot, scraped and chopped
1 parsnip, peeled and chopped
4 large tomatoes, peeled and chopped
2 green peppers, seeded and sliced
1 stick celery, chopped
boiling water

Serves 4

Preheat the oven to 150°C/300°F.

Cut the pork, beef and mutton into bite-sized pieces. Heat the oil in a large heatproof casserole and sauté the meat until it is brown on all sides. Remove the meat and in the same pan fry the rice until it is coated with oil. Replace the meat, season with salt and pepper, sprinkle with paprika and add the bay leaf along with the onions, carrot, parsnip, tomatoes, peppers and celery. Stir gently to mix well. Cover with boiling water and cook in a slow oven for about 2 hours or until the meat is tender.

PITA OD SPANAĆA

500 g spinach, thoroughly washed
250 g fresh ricotta or cottage cheese
30 g grated Parmesan cheese
2 eggs, beaten
2 tablespoons cream or milk
salt and freshly ground black pepper
12 sheets filo pastry
oil or melted butter

Serves 4–6

Preheat the oven to 180°C/350°F and grease a rectangular ovenproof dish.

Cook the spinach in a large pan over a gentle heat (as the spinach retains water naturally you do not need to add water to cook it.) Drain in a colander and squeeze out the excess moisture. Chop finely. In a separate bowl mix the two cheeses with the eggs and cream and season with salt and pepper. Add to the spinach and mix well.

Place a layer of the filo in the bottom of the prepared dish, brush with a little oil, place another layer of filo on top and repeat this procedure until 6 sheets of the filo have been used up.

Cover the pastry with the spinach and cheese mixture and top with the remaining filo, brushing between each layer as before. Brush the final layer with oil and score into pieces with a sharp knife. Bake in a moderate oven until golden. Serve hot or cold.

Both Australia and New Zealand are blessed with an abundance of first-rate fresh food including beef, lamb, fish, shell fish and a large variety of fruit and vegetables. In addition, Australia has exotic tropical fruit and New Zealand, excellent game. Sydney rock oysters are world famous while the stronger-tasting bluff oysters of New Zealand are superb. Both countries have a wide variety of fine shell fish including New Zealand's elusive toheroas, resembling clams and found at the water's edge. Whitebait are also a New Zealand delicacy as are muttonbirds, although the flesh of the latter is oily and is an acquired taste. Kumara, a sweet potato, is a Maori food which has become a part of the diet of New Zealanders.

National cuisines as such have been slow to evolve in either country. The huge influx of immigrants into Australia in the years following the Second World War has dramatically altered and extended the variety of food available, but in New Zealand a more traditional English and Scottish influence prevails.

In both countries, large amounts of red meat are consumed. The barbecue has become an Australian institution and customary fare includes a mixed grill of chops, sausages and steak, accompanied always it seems, with lashings of tomato sauce. Barbecued prawns and carpetbag steak (a thick piece of steak stuffed with oysters) represent a more sophisticated approach to this popular form of outdoor eating.

Australia also boasts several sweets which have gained international recognition. There is for example, the pavlova, made from egg whites and sugar and served with fruit and cream; lamingtons, small squares of sponge cake coated with chocolate icing and rolled in desiccated coconut; and Peach Melba. The latter, although created at the Savoy in London, was first made for the famous Australian soprano and has been adopted by Australians as a national dish.

Beer used to be considered the Australian national drink but during the last three decades the local wine industry has undergone vigorous development and the production of fine wines is now taken very seriously.

DAMPER

Along with billy tea, damper was the basis of Australian bush food. Flour was mixed with water to form a dough which was made into a rough circular shape and cooked in the ashes of the camp fire.

2 cups plain flour
2 teaspoons baking powder
pinch of salt
water
green sticks

Serves 4

Mix together the flour, baking powder and salt. Add enough water to make a sticky dough. Form the mixture into balls around the green sticks. Scrape away the ashes from the centre of the fire and place the damper in the hollow and cover with more ashes. Cooking time will be 30–45 minutes. The damper will sound hollow when knocked. Serve hot.

WHITEBAIT FRITTERS

New Zealanders are primarily red meat eaters and are not given to consuming great amounts of fish. A great delicacy, however, is whitebait, a tiny fish no longer than 4 or 5 cm and netted at the mouth of rivers.

750 g whitebait
boiling water
2 egg yolks
1½ tablespoons plain flour
salt and pepper
2 egg whites
oil for frying
2–3 lemons

Serves 6

Place the whitebait in a wire sieve and wash thoroughly under cold running water. Now pour boiling water over them. Allow to drain while preparing the batter.

Place the egg yolks in a bowl and sift in the flour, stirring until you have a smooth paste. Add a little water if the batter is too stiff. Season with salt and pepper. Whisk the egg whites and fold into the batter, together with the whitebait.

Heat a layer of oil in a heavy based pan and add the mixture, a tablespoon at a time, turning after a few minutes so that both sides are cooked to a golden brown. Drain on absorbent paper and serve at once accompanied by lemon wedges.

YABBIES

A yabby is a type of freshwater crayfish. Many an Australian child has spent happy hours with a lump of 'oldish' meat tied on the end of a piece of string, dangling it into a creek or dam in search of yabbies.

24 yabbies
2.5 litres water
1 teaspoon salt
1 tablespoon sugar
1 tablespoon vinegar

Serves 4

If time permits before cooking soak the yabbies for several hours in a large pan of cold salted water. This will remove the muddy taste from the yabbies. Rinse under cold running water.

In a large pan bring the 2.5 litres of water to the boil and add the salt, sugar and vinegar. Drop the yabbies into the boiling water and cook until they turn pink. Remove and cool in a pan of cold water. Shell and eat with salt, pepper and vinegar, accompanied by bread and butter or damper.

BARBECUED PRAWNS

(AUSTRALIA)

24 large prawns, shelled and de-veined
1 clove garlic, peeled and crushed
1 teaspoon fresh ginger, peeled and
    finely chopped
1 teaspoon brown sugar
½ cup light soy sauce
¼ cup sherry
pinch of chilli powder

Serves 4

Excluding the prawns, mix all the ingredients together. Place the prawns in a shallow bowl and pour the marinade over them. Allow to stand for an hour, turning from time to time. Before cooking the prawns it is important that the barbecue is just glowing coals—the flames must have died away. Cook the prawns for about 5 minutes, or until they turn pink, turning and basting with the marinade from time to time.

RABBIT PIE WITHOUT THE CRUST

(AUSTRALIA)

1 rabbit, jointed
2 onions, peeled and sliced
4 rashers bacon, rind removed
salt and pepper
1 tablespoon plain flour
3 potatoes, peeled and sliced
¾ cup water

Serves 4

Cover the rabbit with cold water and allow to soak overnight. The following day remove and drain off the liquid and preheat the oven to 180°C/350°F.

Place the sliced onions in the bottom of an ovenproof dish, arrange the rabbit on the onions and cover with the slices of bacon. Season with salt and pepper and sprinkle with the flour. Arrange the sliced potatoes overlapping each other on top of the bacon. Pour in the ¾ cup of water, cover and cook in the bottom of a moderate oven for 3 hours. Remove the cover during the last ½ hour of cooking to allow the top to brown.

CARPETBAG STEAK

(AUSTRALIA)

4 pieces rump steak (about 185 g each)
salt and freshly ground black pepper
16 fresh oysters
2 tablespoons oil
½ small onion, finely chopped
1 tablespoon lemon juice
oil for frying
1 tablespoon parsley, finely chopped
2 tablespoons dry sherry

Serves 4

Trim the steak of any surplus fat. With a sharp knife cut diagonally into each piece of steak to form a pocket, taking care not to cut through to the other side. Season the pocket with salt and pepper and stuff each one with 4 oysters. Fasten the pocket together by sewing with a needle and coarse thread, or it can be secured by small skewers.

Make a marinade by combining the oil, onion and lemon juice. Place the steaks in a shallow pan or dish and pour the marinade over them. Allow to stand for 1 hour, turning from time to time.

Heat a little oil in a heavy based pan and cook the steaks, turning to brown both sides. The time taken for cooking will depend on individual taste. Remove the steaks to a warm plate. Add the parsley and sherry to the pan, stir with a wooden spoon to amalgamate the sherry with the juices, pour over the steak and serve at once.

SPICED TAMARILLOS

(NEW ZEALAND)

6 tamarillos, stems and skins removed
boiling water
2 tablespoons cider vinegar
1 teaspoon brown sugar
salt and freshly ground black pepper

Serves 4

Place the tamarillos in a saucepan and pour boiling water over them. Simmer gently until the skin is loose enough to peel off. Remove the tamarillos from the pan, peel and slice them lengthwise. Arrange in a shallow dish, spoon the vinegar over them and season with the sugar, salt and pepper. This dish can be served hot or cold as an accompaniment to roast lamb or beef.

PAVLOVA

6 egg whites
pinch of salt
1½ cups castor sugar
1½ teaspoons cornflour
1½ teaspoons vinegar
1½ teaspoons vanilla essence
**whipped cream, kiwifruit and
    passionfruit for serving**

Serves 6–8

Preheat the oven to 140°C/275°F and grease a 35-cm pavlova tray.

Whisk the egg whites and salt until stiff (they should hold their shape if dropped from a spoon). Gradually add the sugar while continuing to beat. The mixture should look shiny. Still beating add the cornflour, vinegar and vanilla essence. Pile the mixture onto the prepared tray and cook on the bottom shelf of the oven for about 1½ hours, or until the meringue is set. It should not be allowed to brown. Turn the oven off and allow the pavlova to stand until the oven is cool.

When the pavlova is cool, top with whipped cream and decorate with the peeled and sliced kiwifruit and passionfruit.

FRUIT SALAD

1 cup rock melon balls
1 cup diced pineapple
1 cup diced papaw
2 bananas, sliced
1 cup strawberries, hulled
1 apple, unpeeled, cored and diced
1 cup seedless grapes
3 passionfruit

Syrup
¼ cup castor sugar
¼ cup water
**juice of 1 orange or 2 tablespoons
    brandy**

Serves 6–8

First prepare the syrup. Put the sugar and water into a small pan and stir over a low heat until the sugar dissolves. Allow it to come to the boil and remove the pan from the heat and add the orange juice or brandy. Allow to cool while preparing the fruit salad.

Place the prepared fruit in a large glass bowl. Cut the passionfruit in two and scoop out the pulp and add to the fruit. Stir gently to mix. Pour the syrup into the dish and chill. Serve with fresh cream.

ANZAC BISCUITS

1 cup rolled oats
½ cup castor sugar
¾ cup desiccated coconut
1 cup plain flour
1 tablespoon golden syrup
125 g butter
½ teaspoon bicarbonate of soda
1 tablespoon boiling water

Makes 18 biscuits

Preheat the oven to 150°C/300°F and grease a biscuit tray.

Place the rolled oats, sugar and coconut in a large bowl. Sift in the flour and mix well.

In a small pan heat the golden syrup and butter. Mix the bicarbonate of soda with the boiling water and add to the melted butter and golden syrup. Pour this liquid into the bowl containing the dry ingredients and stir until the mixture clings together. Place in small mounds on the prepared tray, allowing room for the biscuits to spread. Bake in the preheated oven for 20 minutes. Remove the biscuits from the oven and cool on a wire rack before storing in an airtight container.

I N D E X

INDEX